AAA Auto Guide

MAKING SENSE
OF
CAR CARE

with
John Nielsen, Director
AAA's Auto Repair Network,
and Steve Bodofsky

AAA PUBLISHING

President & CEO	**Robert Darbelnet**
Executive Vice President, Publishing & Administration	**Rick Rinner**
Managing Director, Travel Information	**Bob Hopkins**
Director, Product Development	**Bill Wood**
Director, Sales & Marketing	**John Coerper**
Director, Purchasing & Corporate Services	**Becky Barrett**
Director, Business Development	**Gary Sisco**
Director, Tourism Information Development	**Michael Petrone**
Director, Travel Information	**Jeff Zimmerman**
Director, Publishing Operations	**Susan Sears**
Director, GIS/Cartography	**Jan Coyne**
Director, Publishing/GIS Systems & Development	**Ramin Kalhor**
Product Manager	**Lisa Spence**
Managing Editor, Product Development	**Margaret Cavanaugh**
AAA Travel Store & E-Store Manager	**Sharon Edwards**
Print Buyer	**Laura Cox**
Manager, Product Support	**Linda Indolfi**
Manager, Electronic Media Design	**Mike McCrary**
Manager, Pre-Press & Quality Services	**Tim Johnson**
Manager, Graphic Communication Services	**Yvonne Macklin**
Project Coordinator	**Sandy Tate**
Technical Advisor	**David Bennett**
Art Director	**Barbra Natali**
Paginator	**Christine Carter**
Illustrator	**David Herrick**
Copy Editor	**Cindy Barth**
Cover Design	**Dunn+Associates Design**

ISBN 1-56251-578-0
Stock Number: 537601

Published by AAA Publishing, 1000 AAA Drive, Heathrow, Florida 32746

Printed in the USA by RR Donnelley & Sons Company

About the Authors and Illustrator

John Nielsen

As director of the automotive services and repair network for AAA, John Nielsen provides strategic vision and direction to AAA's network of 84 clubs across the United States and Canada. He is responsible for developing and managing AAA's vendor relationships, valued at $90 million. Under his leadership, the association's Approved Auto Repair program has grown to 4,600 facilities, which include new-car dealerships and independent repair shops.

John is a mechanical engineer and has spent more than 20 years in management within the automotive industry, serving in marketing, training, customer service, motorsports and product research positions. He holds several Automotive Service Excellence certifications, including master automotive technician, certified truck technician and certified machinist.

Steve Bodofsky

For nearly 20 years, Steve Bodofsky fixed cars . . . as a line mechanic, a lead technician, a shop foreman and a shop owner. He held ASE Master Technician certification as well as Pennsylvania's safety and emissions inspection.

Then, in 1988, he "shifted gears" to become a technical editor and designer for a national automotive francise. Today, as an independent training and marketing developer, Steve writes and designs training programs, magazine articles, marketing literature and websites for a wide variety of companies.

David Herrick

David Herrick specializes in technical and informational illustration for advertising, publishing and marketing. His specialties include artwork for books, magazines, maps, logos and icons.

Table of Contents

Chapter 5 *Ignition and Computer Controls* 59

Once the simplest of systems, today's ignition and computer systems are a marvel of technology, improving economy and power while reducing emissions.

Chapter 6 *Fuel Delivery System: Bringing Fuel to the Engine* 67

Whether it uses gasoline, diesel or another fuel, the delivery system brings that fuel from the tank to the engine.

Chapter 7 *The Cooling System: Taking the Heat* 79

The heat created during combustion can quickly become intense enough to melt metal; that's where the cooling system comes in.

Introduction

For most people, a car is the second-biggest investment they will ever make, right behind their homes. Today's cars tip the scales at $20,000, $30,000, even $40,000. That's a lot of money, even by today's standards.

But very few car owners have any idea of how to protect that investment. Oh, sure, some have an inkling that they should change the engine oil once in awhile. But how often? And what type of oil should they use? Should they change the filter, too?

And what about transmission or brake fluids? Should they be changed, or is that just some kind of con game repair shops play to separate an honest, trusting car owner from his or her hard-earned savings?

The real difficulty here is that today's cars are a far cry from those of just 15 years ago. Over the last several years, we've seen computer controls completely take over engine and transmission operation. And don't forget electronic steering, antilock braking and satellite navigation systems.

Just around the corner, we're hearing about 42-volt electrical systems, fuel cells and hybrid vehicles that operate using both a gas engine and an electric motor. And there's no end in sight. The changes coming down the pike will make the last 10 years look like things were standing still.

So how can you stay ahead of the technology tidal wave? You can't. The object of this book isn't to turn you into an automotive technician. No one book can do that. In fact, by some estimates, today's auto technicians require over a half-million pages of data to perform their jobs efficiently.

Rather, the aim of this book is to help you become more familiar with the car you depend on each and every day. It's to help you develop a workable maintenance routine to keep your car running right for years to come. It's also to help you feel more comfortable when taking your car in for repairs. And it's to prepare you for those times when your car does let you down, so you can get back on the road — fast.

How can you get the most out of this book? First, read it all the way through. You'll probably learn something of value from it that you didn't already know. Then keep it on hand to use as a reference. That way, when you run into a problem or question, you can check out the section that covers the details you're looking for.

Either way, you should find a lot of useful information for buying, fixing and maintaining your car. And that's really the whole idea.

For Your Safety

The engine compartment of a car can be a dangerous place if you aren't careful. Its moving metal parts, spinning belts and superheated fluids can easily cause serious injury or even death. That's why, whenever you open the hood or jack a car up, it's important to follow some basic safety precautions.

1. Always wear appropriate safety eyewear, gloves and a protective apron or coveralls when working under the hood of any car or truck.

2. Never stick your hand near the fan blade or belts while the engine is running or the key is on.

3. Make sure the fan has stopped completely before you reach anywhere near it. Some fans continue to turn for several seconds after you turn the key off. And watch out for electric fans: They can start up without warning, even with the key off.

4. Never try to open the radiator cap while the engine is hot. The coolant temperature can rise over 250° F: hot enough to remove skin. And avoid steam coming from any coolant leaks for the same reason.

5. Never stand over the engine compartment while someone is revving the engine. A fan blade can fly off or can launch some other object.

6. Never stand in front or behind a car or truck with the engine running. The vehicle could drop into gear and run over you.

7. Never try to jump-start a battery that's distorted, frozen or gassing excessively. It could explode and throw sulfuric acid on you.

8. Never smoke or take any ignition source under the hood of a car, whether it's running or not. Flammable vapors can build up from the fuel system or battery and can explode if ignited. For the safest work light, always use a flashlight.

9. Always keep a fire extinguisher handy when working under the hood of a car.

10. Never reach or crawl under a car that's supported by any type of jack. If you must work under a car, always use a set of strong jack stands to hold the car up.

11. Never run a car or truck in a closed garage. Always provide plenty of ventilation to prevent asphyxiation.

12. Always wash your hands thoroughly after working on any part of the car to remove any oils, acids or residues. And if you do get splashed with battery acid, have someone hose you off with water immediately.

13. Be careful not to spill any oils, fluids or additives on the car's paint. If you do, quickly flush the area with water to prevent damaging the finish.

14. Never connect or disconnect any wiring while the key is on, unless you're absolutely sure which system you're working on.

Icons

As you're reading through this book, watch for these icons:

 Indicates a condition that could cause serious personal injury... or even death.

 Indicates a condition that, while not fatal, still could cause personal injury.

 Indicates a condition that could damage property, such as your car or your house.

 Indicates a message you need to know before tackling a test or repair. No one will get hurt, and probably nothing will be damaged, but changes are you won't get the results you're looking for without this tip.

 Indicates a side item you may find interesting. It isn't critical. It's just a good tip you may want to know.

 Indicates a clever way to save money, make your car last longer or get a more effective repair, right from the pros.

Always check these notices carefully when you're reading this book. They could save you time, money and even your life.

CHAPTER

1

In An Emergency

In This Chapter

• • • • • • • • • • • •

- What to do if your car won't start
- How to deal with emergency situations
- How to respond when a warning light comes on

From simple "no-starts" to potentially catastrophic brake failures, this chapter covers information on emergency conditions. Even the best-maintained car eventually will have a problem. Whether it's something as simple as a flat tire or as potentially life threatening as a brake failure, one day your car *is* going to let you down.

That's what this chapter is for: to help you figure out what to do in case of a problem. Whether it's a simple flat tire or your car just won't move, this chapter will help you find the information you need to identify the likely source of the problem and how to deal with it.

In some cases, such as a flat tire, you'll be able to use this as a reference when a problem occurs. Just turn to the section that covers your specific problem and start reading. Other sections — particularly the one that covers brake failures — you'll want to read ahead of time in order to familiarize yourself with the topics covered.

Your Car Won't Start

The phrase "won't start" covers a variety of different problems. It could be something as simple as a battery failure, or your engine could have fallen out of the car — a big difference in problems. So we're going to break this heading into three separate sections:

Because the starting problems can have a variety of symptoms to indicate a completely different problem, each section lists the most common symptoms for a specific failure. Once you find the description that most closely matches your car's problem, read through the explanation and see how to deal with it.

Here are a few other emergency conditions and procedures covered in this book:

What to Do About Warning Lights

Warning lights are difficult to cover from a generic standpoint, because every car uses different lights and strategies. Your car may have a light that says "oil" for oil pressure, and another that says "temp" for coolant temperature. A second car may have a single "engine" light that covers both items.

To make sure you know what each warning light means, carefully read through your owner's manual. So what do you do when a light comes on? That depends on which light it is:

Oil Pressure Light – Indicates you've lost oil pressure in the engine. Pull over and turn off the engine immediately! Not a few miles from now. You may damage the engine severely if you continue to drive the car with the oil light on.

Check the oil level. If it's very low, add oil to bring it to the proper level. Then restart the engine. If the light goes out, you can drive the car, but have it checked for an oil leak or high oil consumption. If the level is OK but the light is still on, leave the engine off and have the car towed. Never drive the car without oil pressure: It doesn't take long to destroy the engine without oil.

Temperature Light – Indicates the engine is running hot. What you do depends on whether your car uses electric cooling fans or not.

Wait for the engine to cool. Make sure the engine stops steaming and the upper radiator hose is soft before attempting any emergency repairs. Once the engine cools and the upper radiator hose is soft, use a rag to open the radiator cap.

If the radiator fluid level is low, check for leaks in the system. If you find a hole in a hose, wrap it with some duct tape for a temporary repair. If the hole is near the end of the hose, cut the end off the hose and clamp the remaining hose back onto the fitting. Start the engine, and slowly fill the radiator with a 50-50 mix of water and antifreeze. Reinstall the radiator cap, but don't lock it all the way. Turn it only halfway to prevent building up pressure.

If the radiator is full, the problem could be a stuck thermostat, an inoperative cooling fan or a blown head gasket. In any case, take your car to the shop to be checked and repaired.

Charging System Light – Indicates the voltage has dropped enough to discharge the battery. As long as the light goes out as soon as you start moving, don't worry too much about it. But have the system checked when you get a chance.

If the light stays on, it indicates a serious problem. If the headlights are off, you'll probably be able to drive to the repair shop. Shut off any unnecessary accessories to keep from draining the battery. If it's nighttime or your headlights stay on all the time, you may not make it to the shop before the battery gets too low to keep the engine running. Stop the car as soon as it's convenient, and call for assistance.

Brake Light — This one is a peculiar warning light because it may indicate more than one problem. It could indicate:

- The emergency brake isn't all the way off.
- There's a pressure loss in the hydraulic brake system.
- The brake fluid is low.

Don't drive the car if the brakes are not working properly! If you suspect there's a problem, pull over and call for assistance.

To isolate the problem, start by checking your emergency brake. Apply and release it a couple of times and see if the light goes out. If your car has an emergency brake pedal, try lifting the pedal while you pull on the release. If the light remains on, you may need brake fluid. If both the emergency brake and brake fluid seem fine, assume the problem is a hydraulic system failure. Don't drive the car until the problem is fixed.

ABS Light — Indicates a problem in the antilock-brake system; the ABS computer has recognized the problem and disabled the ABS system. Your brakes will now operate like hydraulic brakes and you'll be able to stop normally. Just don't slam on the brakes.

Check Engine or **Service Engine Soon** or **Power Loss Light** or **Malfunction Indicator Lamp** — Indicates a problem in the car's computer system. You probably aren't familiar enough with the computer system to identify or isolate the specific problem, but what you should do about it depends on how the light behaves. If the light comes on for a little while and goes out, then you may have a momentary problem in the system. Once the light goes out, the problem is no longer occurring. But it may have caused the computer to store a diagnostic trouble code in its memory. Take the car to your repair shop when you have a chance and ask that the computer system be checked.

If the light comes on and stays on, it indicates an ongoing problem. While the problem may not be severe, it may affect your car's performance, gas mileage and emission levels. Take it to a repair shop as soon as possible. If the light flashes on and off, the car may have a severe problem that will cause additional damage. If your repair shop is nearby, take the car in right away. If not, shut off the car and call for assistance. Some cars have other warning lights beyond those listed here. These lights have a wide range of uses, including a situation as simple as an open door. Your owner's manual has information about all the warning lights in your car — and what to do about them — in detail.

Emergency Phone Numbers

1. Call 9-1-1.
2. Use the roadside emergency call boxes to call for assistance.
3. If you're a member of AAA, call 1-800-AAA-HELP.
4. The hearing impaired and TDD users can call 1-800-955-4833.

CHAPTER

2

Maintenance: The Key to Extending Your Car's Life

In This Chapter

• • • • • • • • • • • •

- How to adjust your car's maintenance schedule to your personal driving characteristics

- The difference between "normal" and "severe" driving conditions

- Introduction to AAA's *Emergency Car Care Guide and Maintenance Log*

A Tale of Two Autos

Two cars come off the same assembly line within minutes of one another. Both are sold on the same day to people who have similar driving styles and drive roughly the same number of miles. You might think both cars should hold up equally well, with similar expenses for repairs over the years.

But, surprisingly, the first car ends up costing its owners far more than the second. Over the years, the first car is less dependable and spends far more time in the shop than the second. It has let its owners down more than once and left them stranded on the highway.

Meanwhile, the second car has provided dependable transportation for years. It starts every morning in the coldest weather. Breakdowns have been virtually nonexistent, and repair costs have been well below the norm.

So what was the difference? Maintenance.

For the first couple of years, both cars held up about the same. But during those years, the second car received regular maintenance, while the first just received gas. The differences really started showing up in the third and fourth years. That's when hoses started getting brittle, belts started cracking, and the oil in the engine turned to sludge in the first car — all because its owners didn't follow the factory maintenance recommendations. Five years down the road, the owners of the first car traded it in. They didn't get much for it, but after all, it *was* 5 years old.

Meanwhile the second car's owners also bought a new car and gave their old car to their teenagers, who continued to drive it for another four years. And when the kids went off to college, they sold the second car for more than the first car's owners received four years earlier.

This story is a fantasy; it never really happened. On the other hand, it happens all the time, with cars all around the world. And each and every day, car owners prove that the key to keeping a car on the road is preventive maintenance, performed at regular intervals based on time or mileage.

Mileage or Time

Whenever you check a car maintenance schedule, you'll see recommendations in both mileage and time. For example, the owner's manual may suggest that you change the oil every "7,500 miles or three months." And if you're like most people, you look at the mileage recommendation and say, "Oh, I only drive about 10,000 miles a year, so I only have to change my oil every nine months or so, right?" Not really.

Take another look at the recommendation: 7,500 miles *or three months.* The three months is the key. What they're saying is that you should change the oil *at least* four times a year . . . every three months. But if you happen to drive more than 30,000 miles a year (4 times 7,500 miles), you should have the oil changed even more often. So, to make sure you're providing the best protection for your car, always check the mileage *and* time recommendations, and then go with the one that's more frequent.

Is Your Driving Normal or Severe?

Another condition of vehicle maintenance schedules is whether your driving is *normal* or *severe*. The intervals listed are always for normal driving conditions. For severe conditions, you're supposed to reduce the time or mileage between maintenance intervals. But what do they mean by normal? And what constitutes severe driving conditions? Let's take a look at two drivers:

The first is an older couple who rarely drive more than 5,000 miles a year. The second is an over-the-road salesman who drives more than 100,000 miles a year. Whose driving would you consider severe?

If you guessed the salesman, sorry. That's the wrong answer. Actually, mile for mile, his car has the easier mileage:

- Every time he starts the car, his engine warms up all the way and burns off any contaminants in the oil.
- His transmission hardly shifts at all, since he's usually on the expressway.
- He drives for miles before he touches his brakes.
- Most of the time he's driving on straight stretches of road, so his tires and suspension get very little workout.

Overall, his car's miles are even easier than normal — it's just that he drives a lot more of them than most people. But what about the other car?

- It rarely warms up all the way before it's shut off, so the oil may become contaminated easily.
- The driving is always stop and go, so the transmission is always upshifting and downshifting.
- The car's always in traffic, so the brakes, tires and suspension get a real workout.

Overall, the miles of the older couple's car are far more severe.

Here's a list of conditions that could be considered severe:

- Short trips and local driving
- Stop-and-go driving

- Sustained high-speed driving
- Extremely cold or hot weather
- Wet, snow-covered or icy roads
- Dirty air, caused by construction or dirt roads
- Excessive idling
- Towing a boat, camper or trailer
- Driving at high altitudes

If your driving consists of any of these special conditions, you should consider your driving conditions as severe and increase your maintenance schedule accordingly.

Maintenance Schedule

Here's a schedule for some of the more common maintenance items necessary, along with an average time and mileage recommendation. You can refer to this schedule as a basic guide for determining when you should perform these maintenance items.

But not every car's maintenance schedule is the same, so always refer to your owner's manual for recommendations specific to your model. And remember to factor in your personal driving habits when determining whether to consider the schedule for "normal" or "severe" conditions.

Service Item	Time	Severe Mileage	Normal Mileage
Lube, Oil Change and Filter	3 Months	3,000	7,500
Wheel Balance	6 Months	6,000	6,000
Tire Rotation	6 Months	6,000	6,000
Wheel Alignment*	1 Year	12,000	12,000
Cooling System Service	2-3 Years	100,000	100,000
Automatic Transmission Service	2-3 Years	24,000	100,000
Air Conditioning System	1 Year		
Inspect and Repair or Replace as Necessary:			
Brakes	6 Months	6,000	6,000
Belts and Hoses*	3 Months	3,000	7,500
Lights	Weekly	NA	NA
Tire Pressure	Weekly	NA	NA
Air Filter*	6 Months	7,500	15,000
Fuel Filter*	2 Years	30,000	60,000

*May vary, based on actual condition of the component.

AAA's *Emergency Car Care Guide and Maintenance Log*

AAA created the *Emergency Car Care Guide and Maintenance Log* to help car owners keep track of their cars' maintenance schedules. Just follow the guidelines in the maintenance schedule and record the maintenance on the record pages. That way you'll always know what's due, to keep your car in top condition.

Maintenance Record

At AAA, we're here to help make your driving experiences safe, secure and comfortable. We believe in preventive maintenance for your car, because research shows that preventive maintenance makes cars last longer.

More than Just Maintenance

If the *AAA Emergency Car Care Guide and Maintenance Log* included just schedules and record pages, it still would be great to keep in your glove box. But that's not all it is. It also includes lots of valuable information for dealing with emergencies. Let's face it, maintenance isn't some kind of silver bullet that protects you from every kind of problem. Accidents still happen; tires still blow out.

That's where the *AAA Emergency Car Care Guide and Maintenance Log* can help. It is straight talk from the automotive experts at AAA, and it puts all sorts of valuable information on emergency situations right at your fingertips. From how to jump-start a battery, to how to change a flat tire, the *AAA Emergency Car Care Guide and Maintenance Log* is a great resource.

And, as a special gift for buying this book, you can get a copy of the *AAA Emergency Car Care Guide and Maintenance Log* absolutely free. Just fill out the reply card in the back of this book and send it in to the address shown.

So don't wait: Send for your free *AAA Emergency Car Care Guide and Maintenance Log* today and start keeping your car in shape right away.

CHAPTER

3

Your Owner's Manual: The Best-Kept Secret for Car Care

In This Chapter

• • • • • • • • • • •

- The importance of reading your owner's manual

- What kind of information is available in the owner's manual

- How to get the most out of the manual

You just brought home your new car. It could be a brand-new vehicle or a used car. There's no question about it, this time you're going to take care of this one. This car's going to last a good long time.

And then it happens — a light on the dashboard comes on. Did you forget to put oil in the engine? Is it overheating? Your old car didn't have a light that said "check engine." Should you pull over and stop the car? There are dozens of different lights and buzzers on many cars. Do you know the difference between them and what each one means?

You want to be familiar with each and every warning light on your car *before* you take it out on its maiden voyage. Every light, every buzzer, every switch, dial and gauge has been listed and carefully explained in your owner's manual. There's a wealth of information in your car's owner's manual.

In this chapter, we'll take a look at your car's owner's manual. We'll see what type of information appears in a typical manual, why that information is important and how to get the most out of your car's manual. Most booklets start with a table of contents. Take a look at yours. The contents page is a great way to learn what the manual covers and where to find it.

Seats and Seat Belts

There's probably a section covering seats, seat belts, air bags (depending on how old your car is) and child safety seats. The owner's manual will have information you need to know before you buy a child seat, including specifications and proper placement, plus vehicle information about maintenance and emergencies. You may find much of this information helpful on a daily basis.

Many vehicle manufacturers have specific instructions or require special equipment for installing child safety seats. The vehicle owner's manual will indicate if you will need "extras" such as a locking clip that secures the vehicle safety belt around the child safety seat or an accessory belt for fitting child seats in particular seating positions. So check your car's owner's manual before purchasing a seat. Look for specifications and proper placement of the child seat.

Of course, everyone knows how to use seat belts, right? But what about if you're pregnant? The manual explains how to adjust the belt to provide proper protection. There's also information about extenders, comfort guides and how to check the seatbelts to make sure they're working properly. There's even something about replacing them after an accident. And that's just on seatbelts.

Instrument Cluster

What about those warning lights we talked about earlier? Are you really sure what you're supposed to do when one lights up? Your owner's manual has a whole section covering the instrument panel — how to work the lights, how to operate the wipers and how to use the climate control system properly. It even goes into detail on each and every warning light and gauge in the car. It tells you what each light means, what causes them to light and what to do when the light comes on.

Driving Practices

But that's not all. Most owner's manuals cover specific driving practices, concepts such as defensive driving, braking, steering and even towing a trailer. And not just from a standpoint of car care. These sections cover practices for safer driving in all sorts of conditions. For example, you may find a section on winter driving that includes how to keep control of your car on snow-covered roads. There's even a list of some of the emergency items you should keep on hand.

Here's something of interest: If your car becomes snowbound, should you keep the engine running? Not a good idea, according to one owner's manual. Seems that as the snow builds up along the sides of the car, it can trap exhaust gasses underneath. Those exhaust gasses can leak into the passenger compartment and end up killing you.

The right thing to do is get out of the car and clear away any snow from the tailpipe and the underside of the car. Then you can start and run the engine for a little while, until the passenger compartment warms up. Once it's warm inside, shut off the engine. This saves fuel, so you can stay warm longer. That's a lot of really good information — information you might never have learned until it was too late.

Emergency Conditions

What do you do if your car's battery goes dead or if a tire goes flat? Or how about if you get stuck in the snow, mud or sand? Do you know how to turn on the emergency flashers?

If you can't answer any of these questions, you probably should read through your owner's manual, since most manuals provide a complete explanation of what to do in case of a problem while on the road. Of course, you're already reading this book. And we're going to cover most of those items here. So why bother reading about them again?

For the specifics: Your owner's manual will cover details specific to your car. For example, in this book, we will cover the proper and safe way to change a tire. But we can't cover exactly where the jack points are on your car, or how to operate the jack or, for that matter, where to *find* the jack in the first place. Those things vary from one car to the next, and your owner's manual is "vehicle specific." It's designed to cover the details of your specific car or truck.

Read It Carefully

"OK," you say, "I'm convinced. I'm going to read my owner's manual. But do I have to read it all the way through, cover to cover?"

Start with the table of contents. Then leaf through the rest of the book and see what catches your eye. You'll be surprised at how much you'll want to read. Then review the owner's manual, one section at a time. There are going to be sections that won't interest you at all. For example, if you're never going to tow a trailer with your car, there's no sense reading about how to do it properly.

But you'll find a lot of information you weren't aware of, from maintenance and instrumentation to driving practices. Read them over carefully. And what about the sections that aren't of interest to you? At least you know they're there, so when the day comes that you do need that information, you'll know where to look.

When you're finished, put the owner's manual back in the glove compartment. That way it's always there — when you need it.

The Engine: The Power to Drive Your Car

In This Chapter

• • • • • • • • • • •

- An introduction to engines in today's cars: how they work and what the differences are

- How to choose the right oil for your car's engine

- What to do if your car loses oil pressure

- The different types of belts and their functions

- How to check the belts and when to have them changed

When you talk about a car's engine, most people immediately think about a gasoline-fired, internal combustion engine. And that's the most common type of car engine on the road today. But it's not the only type: These days there are thousands of cars that run on fuels other than gasoline. Propane, natural gas and diesel engines all have their place on the nation's roadways. And if that isn't enough, over the next few years you'll be seeing a whole new class of cars on the road, based on an electric motor instead of an internal combustion engine. These cars will show up as full electric, gas/electric hybrids and a new design that receives its power from a fuel cell.

In this chapter, we'll take a look at the different types of engines on the road today. We'll see how they work and the differences between them. And then we'll discuss the maintenance many of them need to keep running mile after mile. We'll break these engines into two main categories: internal combustion and electric. Then we'll discuss the differences between each type within those categories.

Internal Combustion Engines

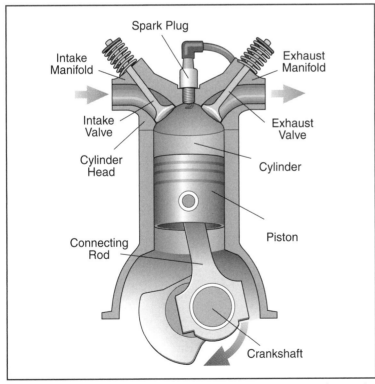

Virtually every gasoline-fired, internal combustion engine on the road today consists of these basic components.

The term *internal combustion* means "burns inside." That's a good description of how the largest segment of engines on the roads today operate. They harness the power of expansion that takes place when a mixture of fuel and air is forced to burn in a confined area. Internal combustion engines can be broken into two subcategories: spark and compression. Spark engines are those engines that use an ignition system to fire the mixture in the engine. *Spark engines* include engines that run on propane, natural gas and. of course, gasoline.

Virtually all spark engines consist of a series of round cylinders, which house a piston and two types of valves to open and close the cylinders. Here's how they work to create power from burning fuel:

A Four-Cycle Engine

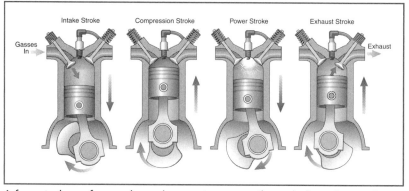

A four-stroke or four-cycle engine creates power through these four cycles: intake, compression, power and exhaust.

The cycle begins with the piston moving downward in the cylinder, and the intake valve open. The downward movement creates a suction, which draws a fuel-and-air mixture in. This is called the *intake stroke*.

When the piston reaches the bottom of its stroke, the intake valve closes. The piston begins moving upward, compressing the fuel-and-air mixture. This is called the *compression stroke*. Compressing the mixture causes it to heat up and increases its volatility (its ability to burn).

When the piston approaches the top of its compression stroke, the ignition system sends a spark to the spark plug. The spark ignites the hot, compressed mixture, which causes it to expand rapidly. This is the combustion part of the internal combustion engine. The mixture burns and expands, forcing the piston down in the cylinder and creating the power in the engine. This is called the *power stroke*.

Once the piston approaches the bottom of the power stroke, the exhaust valve opens. The piston moves upward again, this time forcing the burned fuel-and-air mixture out. The burned gasses continue through the exhaust manifold, and out through the exhaust system. This is the *exhaust stroke*.

When taken together, these four strokes — intake, compression, power and exhaust — make up the four strokes of the four-stroke or four-cycle engine. This is the most common type of engine, and nearly all car engines that operate on gasoline, propane or natural gas work similar to this. There are minor variations in the number of valves and cylinder configuration, but the vast majority of spark-type engines work this way.

The piston connects to a series of cranks, called a crankshaft. This crankshaft turns the up-and-down movement of the pistons into a rotating movement that can be converted into power to turn the wheels.

Compression engine is another term for diesel engine. Diesel engines run without the benefit of a spark to ignite the mixture in the engine. Instead, they use the heat and pressure generated through extreme compression to fire the mixture.

Diesel engines still operate on four cycles, or strokes, and those strokes are identical to those in a spark engine. The difference is that the compression stroke compresses the mixture far more than on a gas engine: more than 20-to-1 compression, as opposed to 8-to-1 on a spark engine. That extreme compression heats up the mixture to the point of auto-ignition: The mixture ignites on its own, without any spark to cause it to fire.

But just as with the spark engine, diesel engines have one main purpose: to convert the expansion of gasses during ignition into power to be sent to the wheels.

More from Less: Turbochargers and Superchargers

The internal combustion engine is a class of pump: the greater the volume going into the engine, the greater the power coming out. So, in general, the bigger the engine, the more powerful it is. But the increased cost and decreased availability of gasoline caused the government to set limits for fuel consumption. These Corporate Average Fuel Economy standards have forced manufacturers to create cars with smaller engines. The problem is, consumers still want power from their cars.

One way that manufacturers addressed this need for more power with better fuel economy was to increase flow through the smaller engines. They did this by adding *turbochargers* and *superchargers* to the engines. These devices are basically small fans that force additional air into the engine.

Turbochargers use the engine's exhaust to power the fan. As the engine speeds up, the exhaust gases flow across one side of the turbo, causing it to spin faster. This fan forces air into the engine under pressure, increasing the flow through the engine.

A supercharger also provides power by increasing pressure entering the engine, but instead of using the exhaust, superchargers use a belt, driven from the engine's crankshaft.

In either case, the additional air enables the engine to create more power, while still working with a smaller engine.

Electric Motors

The high cost of gas, combined with the need to reduce exhaust emissions, has opened a whole new automotive market: the electric car. Electric cars never need gas and never need an emissions inspection. In addition, there are a number of tax rebate programs available to consumers who buy electric cars. Over time, the combination of rebates and reduced expenses could completely offset the initial cost of the car. But there are a number of downside considerations for electric cars:

- Limited Range — Even the best electric cars on the market will only go about 80 to 100 miles before needing to be recharged.
- Limited Speed — Some electric cars only reach 25 mph.
- Limited Power — Acceleration from zero to 60 mph on some electric cars can take up to 30 seconds.
- Limited Features — Most electric cars on the market so far don't offer such things as air conditioning or power steering.

And just because you don't have to buy gas doesn't mean electric cars run for free. You still have to pay for the electricity to charge the batteries. Not to mention that those batteries won't last forever, and replacing them is a fairly substantial expense. To help improve on some of these features, and make electric cars more functional — and more desirable — auto manufacturers have started looking into some new twists on the electric car power plant.

Hybrid Cars

Instead of simply using an electric motor, manufacturers combine an electric motor with a small gas engine to give things a little extra kick. The gas engine provides additional power, increases the overall speed and range, and enables manufacturers to offer more features. But since the gas engine is just a kicker instead of the entire power plant, these hybrid cars can get well over 80 miles per gallon.

Fuel Cells

In 1839, William Grove discovered a way to combine hydrogen and oxygen to create electricity. And instead of poisoning the air, the exhaust is pure water. While new to the automotive market, NASA has been using fuel-cell technology to provide electricity and drinking water for astronauts since the Apollo missions.

Basically containing an onboard recharging system, the fuel-cell cars use a reformer to extract hydrogen from gasoline. The fuel cell combines hydrogen with oxygen from the atmosphere to create electricity to charge the batteries. The exhaust is pure water and can be released safely into the atmosphere.

While still in development as of this writing, look for fuel-cell cars to start showing up on the market over the next few years. As the technology improves, these cars may revolutionize the entire automotive industry.

Engine Oil: Your Car's Lifeblood

As you might expect, the engine oil provides lubrication for the moving components inside internal combustion engines. But that's not all it does. Engine oil fulfills a number of other functions.

To begin with, engine oil captures dirt particles and fuel vapors, and holds them in suspension, away from moving parts inside the engine. It provides additional cooling for some of the components. And it even helps operate the valve train in engines that use hydraulic lifters to open the valves.

With all it does, it's no wonder that regular oil changes are critical for engine durability. In fact, no other maintenance item is so important for extending the vehicle's life and reducing repair costs. Changing the oil has these direct effects for protecting the engine:

- It removes harmful vapors that build up in the crankcase during combustion.
- It eliminates particles of carbon and dirt that build up during normal operation.

Oil Traveling through the Engine

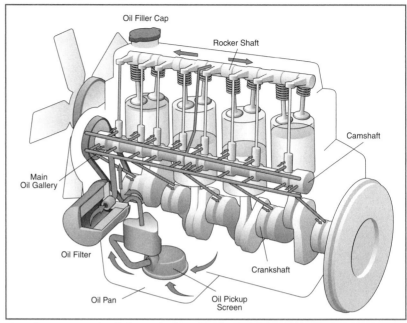

The oil pump sends oil through the oil gallery to lubricate every moving part in the engine.

- It replaces depleted additives designed to reduce friction and wear.
- It renews oil *viscosity*, or thickness, to improve lubrication.

But not all of the benefits of changing oil are due directly to the oil itself. That's because during a typical oil change — the familiar "lube, oil and filter" service — the service technician usually checks a number of other items and performs other services on the car:

- Lubricates the suspension and steering, and checks for obvious wear or damage.
- Examines the underside for leaks or other obvious problems.
- Checks the oil levels in the differential and manual transmission.
- Checks all under-the-hood fluid levels.
- Checks belts and hoses.
- Checks the air filter.

Depending on where you go, the technician may perform several other checks and services as part of a normal oil change procedure. That's why regular oil changes are so important: not just for the new oil — a valuable consideration in itself — but also for the other checks and tests that get performed at the same time.

Choosing the Right Oil for Your Car

When you walk into an auto parts store, go to the aisle where they keep engine oil. There they are, stacked floor to ceiling . . . engine oils as far as the eye can see: single weights, multigrades, high detergent, synthetics, oils specially formulated for older engines, smaller engines, SUVs, high performance. And the list goes on and on, with prices ranging from under a buck, to $4 or $5 a quart.

What do those terms mean? And, more importantly, which oil should you use in your car? To answer the second question, we need to answer the first one, so it is important that you understand a few terms and concepts about engine oil.

Single Weight vs. Multigrades — If you look at the front of any bottle of engine oil, you'll see some large numbers: SAE 30 . . . 10W-40 . . . 5W-50.

Those numbers are the SAE rating for the oil's viscosity. The SAE — Society of Automotive Engineers — has set standards for viscosity; that is, how thick the oil is or, more accurately, how easily the oil flows. The lower the number, the more easily it flows (the thinner the oil). So oil with an SAE rating of 10 will flow more easily than one with a rating of 30.

Oils tend to get thicker (more viscous) in cold weather. Heavier oils can become so thick that the engine won't crank over in cold weather. But when the engine gets hot, thinner oils may not provide enough protection for the engine.

That's why oil manufacturers came out with multigrade oils. These oils have two numbers, which indicate that the oil exhibits the characteristics of both SAE ratings. So an oil with a rating of 10W-30 will flow like a 10 grade oil when it's cold but will remain as thick — or viscous — as a 30 weight when the engine gets hot. The "W" indicates the oil has been tested for cold weather performance.

Gasoline Engine vs. Diesel Engine — Is your engine a gasoline or a diesel engine? Believe it or not, it matters when choosing an oil. On the front of the bottle is a starburst symbol. It indicates whether the oil is designed for use in a gasoline engine or a diesel engine.

What's the difference between a gasoline or a diesel engine? A gasoline engine uses a spark to ignite the mixture in the cylinders. A diesel engine doesn't. Only diesel engines are compression engines; that is, they fire based strictly on compression. They don't use a spark to fire the cylinders.

IMPORTANT

Many oils are approved for both gasoline and diesel engines. These oils will have both an SJ and a CF rating in the API symbol.

Tip Provided by
John Africano
Automobile Club of New York

The starburst only appears on oil recommended for gas engines.

This symbol on the back of the bottle tells you what type of engine the oil is suited for and whether it provides adequate protection for your car's engine.

TECH TIP

There's a myth that suggests you shouldn't use detergent oil in an older engine. These detergents simply hold dirt and carbon in suspension to prevent them from building up inside the engine. As long as your engine has a replaceable oil filter, you can — and should — use detergent oil in your engine.

Tip Provided by
Don Beyer
AAA Washington

The second symbol is the API rating. The American Petroleum Institute developed these ratings to indicate whether the oil is for a gasoline or a diesel engine, plus what level of protection it offers.

See the SJ in the symbol? The S indicates this oil was made for gasoline engines. The J indicates that this oil has the latest additive package and rating available. SA was the first of these ratings — the letters increase with each upgrade to the specs. SJ oil is approved for use in all gasoline engines, with rating requirements from SA through SJ.

Oils designed for diesel engines have a C code. CF is the latest rating and is approved for all diesel-type engines.

Detergent Oils — Many oils are quick to display the fact that they're *detergent oils* right on the bottle. This might lead you to believe that oils without that statement aren't detergent oils. Nothing could be further from the truth.

The fact is, virtually every multigrade oil also is a detergent oil. Only single-grade oils, such as straight 30-weight oils, are non-detergent. Should you be using a detergent oil? The simple answer is yes. In most cases, your car should use a detergent oil. The only exceptions are engines that don't have an oil filter. That usually means lawnmower engines. The last common car to have an engine without an oil filter was the Volkswagen Beetle — the *old* one, not the new one.

Synthetic vs. Standard — To hear some folks tell it, synthetic oils are a magic elixir. Use it in your engine, and you'll get a half-million miles out of your engine without ever having to change your oil again. That may be overstating things just a bit. The truth is, synthetic oils do provide better lubrication and can increase the life of your engine substantially. But there's nothing to indicate you can or should increase the time between oil changes.

What's more, if your car's engine is a little on the worn side or leaking slightly, there's a good chance that it'll burn or leak more with synthetic oil in the crankcase. That's because synthetic oils tend to be somewhat less viscous (thinner) than standard oils, due in part to their smaller molecular structure. So while synthetics can work their way into smaller areas and provide better lubrication, the same properties can cause the oil to leak or burn more easily.

Should you use synthetic oil in your car? If your engine is fairly new, synthetic oil will provide excellent protection against wear. But realistically, so will sticking to a good maintenance schedule and using a good quality, organic-based oil.

OK, now that you know about the different types of engine oils, which one should you choose for your car's engine? That's easy: Open your owner's manual and see what the manufacturer recommends. Chances are it'll have a few recommendations, depending on the average temperature where you drive. If you live in an area where it gets cold in the winter, you'll probably want to choose the lighter grade of oil for winter driving. Then, when the weather warms up, you can switch to the heavier grade.

For example, say your owner's manual suggests a 5W-30 or 10W-30, depending on the average temperature. In the winter you'll probably want to use the 5W-30 oil and switch to the 10W-30 in the warmer weather. If the weather remains fairly warm where you are, you probably can stick with the heavier oil year-round. On the other hand, if you live in a colder climate, you'll probably want to go with the 5W-30.

Next, check the API rating. If your car has a spark engine — which means it uses gasoline, propane or natural gas — look for an oil with an SJ or higher rating. If you're driving a diesel, it should have a CF rating or higher.

Using Engine Oil Additives

About one aisle over from the engine oils in the auto parts store is an entire aisle dedicated to oil additives. These additives usually fall into one of five categories:

- Thickeners
- Friction reducers
- Cleaners
- Stop leaks
- Magic cure-alls

Should you use any of these in your engine? In most cases, no. As long as your engine is running OK, you have no need for them. Let's take a quick look at each category.

Thickeners — These are the heavy, gooey additives that barely seem to flow in the bottle. The object of these additives is to thicken the oil, which, by definition, reduces leaks and oil burning, and increases oil pressure. These additives work, but remember: All they're doing is overcoming engine wear. They may buy you some time, but they won't fix anything.

Friction Reducers — These tend to be the expensive ones, which claim to plate the inside of the engine with Teflon or chrome or graphite. Don't waste your money. If your engine needed to be plated with Teflon, chrome or graphite, it would have come that way from the manufacturer.

Cleaners — They claim to loosen and remove built-up carbon from behind the rings and lifters, which stops oil burning and eliminates engine noise. They may help a really dirty engine, but if you change your oil regularly you shouldn't need them.

Stop Leaks — In most cases these additives are designed to soften seals and cause them to swell up. The concept is good, but they don't usually work.

Magic Cure-Alls — These fall in the category of "if it sounds too good to be true, it probably is." Stay away from anything that claims to be an "engine rebuild in a can."

In the end, the best way to keep your engine in good condition is to change the oil regularly and use a good quality oil. If you do that, you should never need to consider the additive route.

Replace the Filter with Every Oil Change

Many people still believe in replacing the oil filter during every *other* oil change. They figure they're saving money on the filter, plus the extra oil. But what are they really saving? If they change their oil four times a year, that's two filters and a quart or two of oil they end up saving. At today's prices, that works out to somewhere between $15 and $20 a year.

But what are they giving up? To begin with, the old oil filter is at least partially clogged — not a good thing. What's more, they're leaving about 20 percent of the old, dirty oil in the engine. That can't be good. So for a savings of $20 or less a year — or about *5 cents a day* — they're risking the most expensive single component on their cars — the engine.

As an old ad used to say on this very subject, "You can pay me now, or pay me later." Pay them now: Replace the filter every time you have the oil changed.

Checking the Oil

Nothing can damage an engine faster than running it without adequate oil. That's why it's a good idea to check the oil level at least once a week. It's easy to do; all you need is a rag or paper towel.

Here's how to check your car's engine oil, in just *10 easy steps:*

Step

1 Park the car so it is level.

2 Start the engine and let it run until it reaches normal operating temperature. (If it's already warmed up, you can skip this step.)

3 Shut off the engine.

4 Open the hood.

5 Locate the engine oil dipstick and pull it out of the engine.

Checking the Oil Level

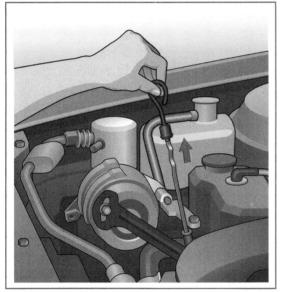

Make sure you check the right dipstick for the engine oil, and pay attention to where it came from, so you can put it back without any problem.

Pay attention to where the dipstick came from, so you can put it back a few steps from now.

Tip Provided by
Randy Loyk
Alberta Motor Association

6 Wipe off the dipstick, using the rag or paper towel.

7 Look at the stick to learn where the *ADD* and *FULL* marks are.

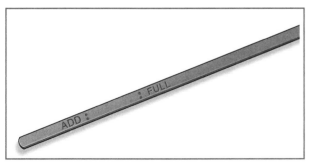

The oil level should be somewhere between ADD and FULL.

8   Slide the dipstick back into the dipstick tube. Make sure it seats all the way down in the tube.

9   Pull the dipstick back out and look for the oil level. Compare the oil level to the marks on the dipstick. If the level is OK, go to step 10.

If the oil is at ADD or below:
- Remove the oil fill cap and pour the needed amount of the proper type of oil into the crankcase.
- Recheck the oil level (steps 6 through 9). Repeat this procedure until the oil is between the *ADD* and *FULL* marks.
- Reinstall the oil fill cap. Make sure it's on properly and tightened securely. Then go to step 10.

10   Replace the dipstick. Make sure you seat it all the way into the tube. Then close the hood.

Keep in mind that most cars today shouldn't use more than a quart or two between oil changes. If you find yourself adding oil every time you fill the tank, take your car to the shop and have them check why it's using oil.

Adding Oil to the Engine

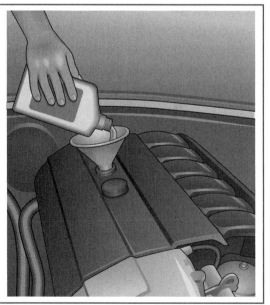

If the oil level's too low, add enough oil to bring it to the proper level.

If the Engine Loses Oil Pressure

You can tell that your car's engine lost oil pressure one of three ways:

1. The oil light comes on and stays on.
2. The oil pressure gauge drops to zero.
3. You hear a loud tapping or knocking from the engine compartment.

If you suspect your engine lost oil pressure, pull over immediately and shut off the engine. Check the oil level. If it's very low, add oil to bring it back to the proper level. Then restart the engine. If the light goes off now, you can drive the car, but get it to a shop to have it checked for an oil leak.

If the level is OK but the light is still on, you'll need to have the car towed. Never drive the car without engine oil pressure: You won't have to drive far before your engine is destroyed.

Drive Belts

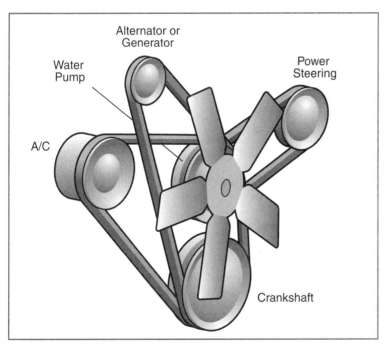

Engines use drive belts to operate different accessories and components such as the water pump, alternator, power steering and air conditioning.

When we talk about a belt on an engine, we're talking about a loop of rubber with a woven reinforcement. The technical term for this is a *drive belt*. The purpose of a drive belt is to transfer the rotation of the engine's crankshaft to an accessory or component to cause it to turn.

For example, the water pump is a component that uses the rotation of the crankshaft to pump coolant through the engine. To transfer the rotation from the crankshaft to the water pump, manufacturers use a drive belt that runs between the two.

An example of an accessory that operates with a belt is the air conditioning compressor. A drive belt provides the rotation the compressor needs to pump refrigerant through the A/C system and transfer heat from the passenger compartment to the air outside.

But that's not all. Some manufacturers use a belt to time the crankshaft to the valves that open and close the cylinders. This is called a *timing belt*, and it uses a series of ridges or cogs to maintain the exact relationship between the camshaft and the crankshaft.

Belts provide many important functions in the operation of your car's engine. That's why it's important to check them to make sure they're in good condition. In this section, we'll cover the different types of belts: how to identify them, how to check them and when to have them replaced.

On most engines, drive belts mount on the front of the engine. They run between two or more pulleys, which hold the belts in line, and enable the belts to drive the accessories and components mounted to the engine. Drive belts operate any or all of these devices, depending on your particular car:

- Water pump
- Cooling fan
- Alternator or generator
- Power steering pump
- Air conditioning compressor
- AIR pump (emission device)

Drive belts come in two main configurations: V-belts and serpentine belts. We'll look at both of these types of belts and see how to identify them, how they work, and how to check them for tension and condition.

V-Belts

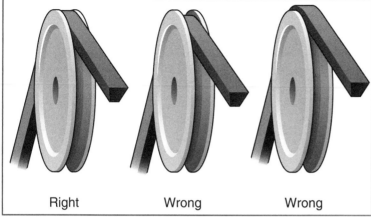

| Right | Wrong | Wrong |

V-belts should ride flush with the top of the belt groove. Too high or too low in the groove could cause the belt to fail.

V-belts take their name from their shape. They're wide at the top and thin at the bottom, forming a wedge or the letter V.

V-belts drive the components and accessories by running through a couple of pulleys that have a V-shaped groove running through them. When pulled tight, these belts connect the accessories to the crankshaft. Then, when the crankshaft turns, it turns the accessory with it.

V-belts come in several different lengths and widths. Both of these differences are important when choosing the right belt for the application. The length of the belt determines whether the belt will reach around the proper pulleys and still be pulled tight.

But the width also is important: It determines whether the belt will fit properly in the groove in the pulleys. When installed properly, the belt should ride flush with the top of the pulley, without any gaps between the pulley and the belt. If the belt rides too low or doesn't fit right between the sides of the pulley, it could twist in the grooves and fail. If it rides too high on the grooves, it will wear unevenly and tear itself up.

Serpentine Belts

Serpentine belts are wide, flat belts, with a series of grooves along the drive side. They're called *serpentine* because they snake back and forth around several different pulleys to drive several different accessories and components at the same time.

The reason serpentine belts have become so popular with manufacturers is because they provide more driving force than a V-belt, with less tension on the component. This reduces the wear on the component bearings, so they're likely to last longer.

The downside is cost. In general, serpentine belts cost more than V-belts. But on the other hand, since they drive more than one component, a single serpentine belt may replace as many as three or four belts, so the overall cost evens out. But if a serpentine belt breaks, all other functions are lost, too.

Belt Wear

There are a number of types of wear to look for when checking a drive belt.

- Cracks — breaks in the drive side of the belt.
- Peeling — extended cracks or breaks in the drive side of the belt, causing sections to lift away. A peeling belt may have whole sections missing.
- Glazing — extremely shiny contact area, which may have been caused by slipping, that can cause additional slipping or noise while operating.
- Fraying — part of the reinforcement or backing hanging off of the belt.
- Oil Contamination — wet or spongy feel to the belt, caused by an oil leak or spill. The leak must be repaired and the oil cleaned up before replacing the belt, or the problem will recur.

If a drive belt exhibits any of these types of wear, you should have it replaced to prevent it from breaking and leaving you stranded.

Types of Damage to Belts

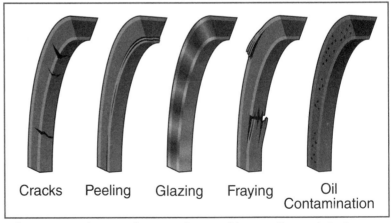

Cracks   Peeling   Glazing   Fraying   Oil Contamination

Belt wear can take many forms, such as cracking, peeling and glazing. You should always replace worn belts to prevent a failure on the road.

Checking Belt Tension

To operate properly, belts have to be tight. Loose belts let the component slip, reducing its efficiency while glazing the belt. On the other hand, if the belts are too tight, they can damage bearings or wear out too quickly.

In the shop, technicians often use a belt tension gauge to check and adjust belt tension. But if you don't have a tension gauge, there are a couple of easy tests you can perform to determine whether a belt is close to the proper tension.

V-Belt Tension

- Grab the belt near the center of the longest run between two pulleys.
- Pull up and down on the belt with medium force.

The belt should deflect between a half-inch (1.25 centimeters) to an inch (2.5 centimeters) in either direction.

Serpentine Belt Tension

- Grab the belt near the center of the longest run between two pulleys.
- Twist the belt gently.

The belt should only twist 90 degrees in either direction. If the belt appears loose, take your car into the shop to have it checked and tightened properly.

Never reach near the belts with the engine running. You could easily lose a finger or even your entire hand. Always make sure the engine's off before reaching into the engine compartment.

Tip Provided by
Earl Baker
AAA Oregon/Idaho

Replacing the timing belt before it breaks can save you a lot more than the time for a breakdown. Some engines don't have adequate clearance between the cylinder head and the pistons. So if the valves are open when the piston comes to the top of the cylinder, the two will hit. If the timing belt breaks on an engine without enough clearance, the valves could bend, leaving you with an expensive repair bill.

In addition to replacing the belts, find out from your repair shop whether your car uses idler pulleys or tensioners for the belts. Very often you can have the bearings replaced in these pulleys or tensioners for only a few dollars while the belts are already off. If yours is one, have that taken care of at the same time.

Tip Provided by
Steven Benedict
AAA of Tidewater Virginia

Timing Belt Keeps the Engine Running

For an engine to run, the pistons and valves have to operate at just the right time, relative to one another. Many of today's cars use a timing belt to link the crankshaft and camshaft timing.

There's no way you'll be able to check the timing belt. It's pretty well buried under a series of covers and shrouds. So you won't know if the belt's beginning to wear — until it's too late.

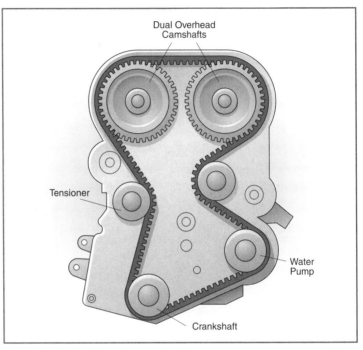

The timing belt drives the camshaft in a synchronized manner with the crankshaft.

That's why most manufacturers recommend replacing the timing belt at regular intervals. Check your owner's manual. If your car's engine uses a timing belt, you'll find the replacement recommendation there. In most cases, the replacement interval will be about five years or 75,000 miles.

In some engines, the timing belt doubles as the drive for the water pump. If your car's engine uses the timing belt to drive the water pump, you should have the pump replaced with the timing belt. This saves you having to deal with an additional repair later, and in most cases the shop won't charge any extra labor to replace the pump, since they already have it off.

Belts as a Maintenance Item

When should you replace the belts? Just when they break or become damaged? Or should you consider them a regular maintenance item? Most manufacturers suggest regular belt replacement, even if they appear OK.

That's because belts wear out, and not all belt wear is completely obvious. And remember, a broken belt can simply be an inconvenience, or it can leave you stranded.

To prevent being stranded by a broken belt, have your car's drive belts replaced at the same time you have the hoses replaced: every four years or 60,000 miles. If your car has a timing belt, check your owner's manual. Most provide a maintenance replacement interval. If your car's owner's manual doesn't, plan on having the belt replaced about every five years or 75,000 miles.

Remember that the idea of maintenance is to prevent breakdowns. One way to keep your car on the road is to replace the belts regularly.

If a Drive Belt Breaks

Would a broken belt keep you from driving the car? It depends on which belt it is. For example, if the belt only drives the air conditioning compressor, then a broken belt won't keep you from driving. You may not be very comfortable, but you'll still be able to drive the car.

If it's the power steering belt, that's a little different. Without the steering belt, the car will be hard to steer. You can still turn the wheels, but you'll really have to pull on the steering wheel. Whether you can continue driving depends on how strong you are. If you can steer the car, you can continue driving until you get to a repair shop.

But if the alternator belt breaks, you may have a problem. If it's daytime and your headlights aren't wired to light all the time, you may be able to drive over to the repair shop. But if it's night or the lights come on whenever you start the engine, you may not get very far before the battery gets too low to run the engine.

And if the belt drives the water pump, forget it. You won't get more than a mile or so before the engine begins to overheat. If you can see the repair shop from where you're sitting, you may be able to make it there on your own power. If not, pull over and call for roadside assistance.

Ignition and Computer Controls

In This Chapter

• • • • • • • • • • •

- An introduction to ignition systems, from early points-and-condenser systems to today's computer controls

- Do cars still need a tune-up?

- What to do if the malfunction indicator lamp lights

To turn air and fuel into power, the mixture has to burn. That's where the ignition system comes in. The ignition system creates a spark to ignite the mixture, which causes the expansion with the cylinders. That's what the ignition system did on the very first car built over 100 years ago. And that's what the ignition system does today. But today's ignition system is a far cry from the ones used on those first cars that started a transportation revolution.

Most of today's cars use a distributorless ignition system. The computer monitors crankshaft position and engine operating parameters through a series of sensors, and then fires the cylinders directly, through a series of individual coils. Fewer moving parts means less wear, and computer control enables the system to adjust for changing conditions thousands of times per second.

But in the end, the ignition system still fires a spark across a spark plug, which ignites the mixture in the cylinder. That much, at least, hasn't changed in over a century of automotive technology.

Distributorless Ignition System

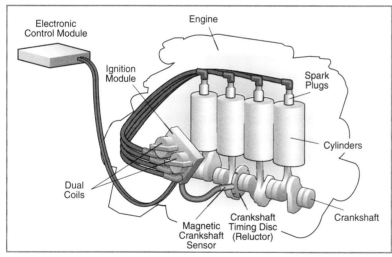

Many cars use a distributorless ignition system, which uses multiple coils that fire two spark plugs at the same time.

Closed Loop Feedback Systems

As fuel economy and emission standards began tightening in the late '70s and early '80s, manufacturers needed a way of controlling engine operation more efficiently. Their answer was closed loop feedback. That sounds like a complex system, but in reality you've been familiar with closed loop feedback for years, in all sorts of applications.

Closed loop feedback simply means a system of sense and adjust: The system senses the conditions taking place, and adjusts to compensate for those conditions.

Your home is filled with devices that operate using a system of sense and adjust. Your refrigerator, freezer, oven and home heating system all work this way. Here's what that means, using your home's heater as an example:

Your home has a heating system, with a thermostat designed to control its operation. Suppose you set the thermostat to 70 degrees. If the temperature drops below about 68 degrees, the thermostat turns the heater on. The heater runs until the temperature reaches about 71 degrees, then the thermostat shuts it off.

The thermostat constantly monitors the room temperature, sensing when it gets below or above the temperature you selected. It senses changes in temperature, and operates the heater to adjust that temperature as necessary. This system of sense and adjust is a simple, closed loop feedback system.

Today's cars use a closed loop feedback system to control engine operation, but instead of operating on temperature, they operate based on the exhaust. If the engine is running rich (too much fuel), the exhaust will be rich. The computer system senses that through an electronic device called an oxygen sensor.

If the computer senses the exhaust is rich, it reduces the fuel entering the engine, leaning the mixture. Then, when the oxygen sensor indicates the mixture has become lean, the computer enriches the air/fuel mixture to compensate.

But the computer system doesn't stop with measuring the exhaust. These feedback systems also monitor several other engine and transmission parameters, including temperature, load, and various component positions, to tailor engine performance for every possible contingency.

This constant sense-and-adjust operation enables the computer system to control engine operation to a high level of accuracy. This improves performance and economy, while reducing emissions.

Diagnostic Trouble Codes

Any system as complex as the engine control system in today's cars has a serious downside: How to identify and isolate problems in the system. These systems have several sensors and dozens of connectors and miles of wiring. A single loose connection can cause all sorts of problems, and take hours to identify.

To help technicians find problems, computer control systems usually provide diagnostic trouble codes (DTCs) to indicate problem areas.

Don't get the wrong idea: Diagnostic trouble codes don't diagnose the problem completely. Instead, they indicate problem areas, and show the technician where to look for a problem. The technician still needs to know how to examine electrical circuits to identify the specific cause of the code; it just points the technician in the right direction.

For example, say the computer provides a code for the throttle position sensor. That doesn't necessarily mean the sensor is bad: It could just have a bad connection or be out of adjustment. The code tells the technician which circuit to check; it's up to the technician to test that circuit and iden-tify the specific failure.

The Tune-Up

It wasn't so long ago that a tune-up was like the rings on a tree: You could determine a car's age by counting the number of tune-ups it had received. But what *is* a tune-up? What does it involve? And is it really still necessary? These questions — and many more just like them — have been getting a lot of press lately, mostly because of this one simple misconcep-tion: *When a car isn't running right, a tune-up will fix it.*

It's no real surprise that most people believe this to be true, because in many cases it works out that way. Let's face it, during a tune-up, the techni-cian replaces part of the ignition system. If that part is damaged or worn out, the car's going to run better afterward.

What's more, if you think back several years ago, a tune-up involved a lot more than it does now. Back then, the better part of the car's ignition system got replaced during a typical tune-up. The rest of the system was checked, and anything that was worn or damaged was replaced.

And that's not all. During a tune-up, the technician also would replace several filters, clean out the carburetor and choke, and perform a number of adjustments to the engine. No wonder the car tended to run better afterward.

The Tune-Up Then and Now

But even in the days when a tune-up involved so much, it still was really just maintenance. The fact that it might have corrected a performance problem often was just coincidence. A tune-up on one of today's cars is far less involved than those of yesteryear. The technician replaces the spark plugs, checks the plug wires and maybe replaces a filter or two. That's about it. Today's tune-up is even less likely to correct a performance problem.

In fact, if a tune-up actually corrects a problem with your car's performance, chances are you've been ignoring the maintenance schedule. That's because, with today's computer controls, cleaner-burning fuels and hotter spark, the plugs and filters have to be pretty bad to cause a problem that you'll notice while driving.

So does that mean you no longer need a tune-up? Not really. A tune-up — then and now — still is an important part of a regular maintenance schedule, on any gasoline-type engine. A properly tuned engine will provide better gas mileage, more power and lower emissions. And it will help prevent the catalytic converter from overheating, caused by a misfire or excess emissions.

What Does a Tune-Up Include?

What's included in a basic tune-up depends on the specific engine and its configuration. Virtually every tune-up includes these parts and services:

- Replace the spark plugs.
- Check the ignition system visually and electronically (using an engine analyzer) and repair or replace the components necessary.
- Check the air filter and replace if necessary.
- Check the fuel filter and replace if necessary.
- Check the base idle and adjust if necessary (where it's adjustable).
- Check base timing and advance; adjust if necessary (where it's adjustable).
- Check the knock sensor for proper operation; repair or replace as necessary.
- Clean the PCV system; replace the PCV valve and any filters.
- Analyze the exhaust for proper combustion.
- Check the oxygen sensor and replace if necessary.

Notice there aren't a lot of items that get replaced automatically anymore. That's because most of the systems on today's cars are designed to last 100,000 miles or more. But just because they're designed for it doesn't mean they're *going* to last that long. That's why it's important to have these systems checked, and repaired or replaced as necessary.

Notice, too, that many of the familiar adjustments, such as idle speed and ignition timing, aren't necessarily adjustable any more. Today, the computer handles a lot of those adjustments, so they don't usually wander off of specs. If they aren't right, it's usually due to a problem somewhere in the computer system or engine.

If your car's engine has a distributor, a few other items will have to be checked or adjusted:

- Distributor cap
- Ignition rotor
- Ignition primary pickup and reluctor

And if you still have a car that uses the old points-and-condenser ignition, they should be replaced and adjusted as well. But regardless of what year car you're driving, a tune-up still is an important part of your regular maintenance schedule.

If the Malfunction Indicator Lamp Comes On

The malfunction indicator lamp indicates a problem in the car's computer system. The exact nature of the problem isn't all that important right now: That's for your repair shop to determine. But what you should do about it depends on how the light behaves.

1. If the light comes on for a little while and goes out, then you may have a momentary problem in the system. Once the light goes out, the problem is no longer occurring. But it may have caused the computer to store a diagnostic trouble code in its memory. Take the car to your repair shop when you have a chance and ask that the computer system be checked.

2. If the light comes on and stays on, it indicates an ongoing problem. While the problem may not be severe, it may affect your car's performance, gas mileage and emission levels. Take it to a repair shop as soon as possible.

3. If the light flashes on and off, the car may have a severe problem that will cause additional damage. If your repair shop is nearby, take the car in right away. If not, shut off the car and call for assistance.

Remember the precise conditions taking place when the light came on. Were you accelerating or cruising? Did you just start the car or had it been running for a while? By detailing the conditions, you'll make it easier for the technician to identify the source of the problem.

Tip Provided by
Tom Francois
AAA Colorado

If the malfunction indicator lamp comes on, take your car into the repair shop, but don't shut off the engine. Some codes don't store in memory. If you shut off the engine, the code may clear, and your repair technician will have a difficult time trying to identify the problem.

Tip Provided by
Tom Giasson
AAA Northern New England

CHAPTER

6

Fuel Delivery System: Bringing Fuel to the Engine

In This Chapter

• • • • • • • • • • • •

- Understanding the differences between carburetors and fuel-injection systems

- Choosing the right grade of gas for your car

- What filters should be replaced and when

- The truth about fuel system servicing procedures

Every internal combustion engine needs fuel and air to run. That's the job of the fuel delivery system: combining the right amount of fuel with the right amount of air to keep the engine running. There are several different types of internal combustion engines, including those that run on gasoline, diesel, propane and natural gas. In most cases, propane and natural gas cars strictly are used for fleets and don't find their way into the consumer market. So we'll skip discussing them here.

Most cars that are available to the consumer market run on either gasoline or diesel. We'll look at the details on each type of system and learn how to take care of them.

Carburetor or Fuel Injection?

Fuel delivery systems come in two types: carburetor or fuel injection. Most of the cars on the road today use some type of fuel injection, but there still are plenty of carburetors out there. In simplest terms, a carburetor is a metering device. It redirects air flowing through the engine and takes advantage of the air's movement to regulate the amount of fuel that it delivers.

Carburetor

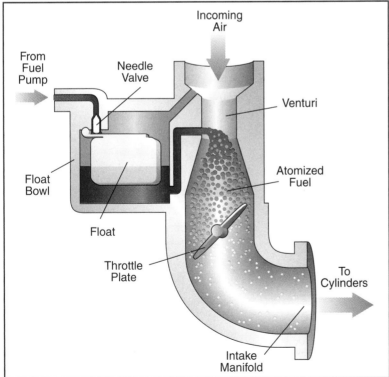

In the past, most cars used a carburetor to deliver fuel to the engine. These carburetors worked well but weren't all that efficient.

The air moving through the carburetor creates a suction to draw fuel through a series of openings called "jets." These jets allow just the right amount of fuel to mix with the air and allow the engine to run.

In later years, manufacturers added computer metering to the carburetors to control fuel more accurately. But even with computer control, carburetors tend to be somewhat wasteful with fuel. That's why most manufacturers now use some type of fuel injection system.

Fuel injection uses one or more nozzles — called injectors — to deliver a carefully measured amount of fuel to the engine. This is a more precise method of delivering fuel. In some cases, the system actually varies fuel delivery on a cylinder-by-cylinder basis.

·Virtually all of today's gasoline-powered fuel-injected cars use computer controls to measure fuel delivery. This provides better fuel economy, quicker response, lower emissions and better performance than a carburetor ever could.

Fuel Injection System

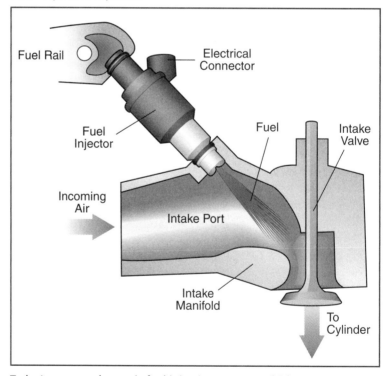

Today's cars use electronic fuel injection systems, which are more efficient than carburetors and allow the engine to provide more power at lower emission levels.

Diesel engines always are fuel injected. Until recently, this fuel injection usually was mechanically controlled. But new emissions and fuel economy requirements have given rise to a new type of diesel engine with full computer controls, including electronic fuel injection.

But there's a downside to electronic fuel injection, in both gas and diesel engines. There's a high level of precision required. Some of today's injectors work with clearances less than half the thickness of a human hair. With tolerances this tight, even the smallest amount of dirt or deposits can have a dramatic effect on engine performance. That's why fuel system maintenance becomes critical on today's cars.

In this section, we'll start by examining the different types of fuels available and learn how to determine which one is right for your car. Then we'll discuss the maintenance necessary for your car to run right.

Different Grades of Gasoline

One of the most obvious differences between gasoline and other types of fuels used in today's cars is that gasoline comes in a number of different grades. Pull into any gas station, and you'll see names like "economy," "regular," "super," "premium" and "high test."

The real problem is that these names vary, with no real consistency, from station to station. So how can you tell whether you want super or premium? Regular or economy? Extra or high-test? Start by ignoring the names. Look at the numbers. All gasolines carry a number known as the *octane rating*. This is a rating of its ability to resist detonation or "pinging." The higher the number, the greater the fuel's resistance to pinging.

So you pull into a typical gas station, and it offers three grades of gasoline:

- A base grade with an octane rating of 87
- A medium grade with an octane rating of 89
- A premium grade with an octane rating of 92

Don't use premium or midgrade fuel if your vehicle was designed to run on 87. There's no benefit to the engine or its performance.

Tip Provided by
Pete Candela
AAA Auto Club South

How do you know which one's right for your car? Check the owner's manual. It lists which octane your car's engine was designed to use to provide the best combination of power, economy and low emissions. In most cases, that's going to be about an 87 octane, though some higher-performance cars may require 89 or 92 octane.

But what if your car pings on 87 octane gas? Under acceleration or with a heavy load, a light ping may be normal. A heavier or more consistent knock indicates a problem in the engine; take it in to your repair shop and have it checked. In most cases, you shouldn't have to increase the octane rating to eliminate a ping.

Cetane: Octane for Diesels

Diesel fuels also have a rating to indicate their ability to sustain combustion. Called the *cetane* rating, it works just like the octane rating in gasoline. The higher the cetane rating, the slower and more completely the fuel burns. Most manufacturers build their diesel engines for a cetane rating of about 43.

What's different about diesel fuels is that in most cases you don't have a lot of choice about which one to use. Gas stations have one grade of diesel. Your choice is either to use it or not. And that's exactly what you should do. If your car doesn't run right on the diesel from one gas station, try another station's diesel. See if it runs any better.

If you can't find a fuel that makes your car run properly, you may have a problem with carbon buildup. Take your car into the shop and have it checked and cleaned. If everything else is OK, there are a couple of diesel fuel additives available to increase the effective cetane level of the fuel. But save them for a final alternative, after trying everything else first.

Are Fuel Additives Necessary?

There are dozens — maybe even hundreds — of fuel additives on the market, with promises of more power, better gas mileage and lower emissions. Do they work? Sometimes. Are they necessary? In most cases, no.

Gasoline Additives

Today's gasolines provide most of the detergents, stabilizers and other additives necessary for most cars to run properly. But there are a few exceptions:

- If you live in a colder region, you may want to add gas line antifreeze (dry gas) to your gas tank. In most cases it isn't necessary, but it can't hurt, and it's a cheap way to provide yourself with some peace of mind.
- If you drive an older car — pre-1975, without a catalytic converter — you may need to use a "lead replacement" additive to provide additional lubrication to the engine's valves. Newer engines use valves designed to hold up without the lead additive.
- If your car sits for months at a time without being run, you might want to add a gas stabilizer to the tank. This prevents the gas from breaking down and going bad.

Those are about the only additives you might have to consider for a gasoline engine.

Diesel Fuel Additives

Diesel engine owners have an entirely different set of problems to consider. To begin with, there are certain microbes that feed on diesel fuels. These microbes come in three basic varieties: bugs (bacteria), plants (algae) and fungus (fungus).

As these microbes grow, they create a slime that blocks up the fuel system. Once that happens, the only repair is to flush the system completely. There are no additives to dissolve or eliminate this slime. To prevent the bugs, plants and fungus from taking hold, there are additives designed to scavenge any water in the tank. This causes the microbes to dry up and die, and prevents them from getting a foothold on your car's fuel system.

Another problem with diesel engines is they're often built for fuels with higher cetane levels than are available at the pump. To combat this, additives are available that increase the effective cetane level by 3 or 4 points, so the engine will run better.

Finally, diesel fuels have problems with cold weather. At low temperatures, diesel fuels thicken up and won't flow properly. Most fuel companies supply the necessary additives in the winter to lower the "pour point" of their fuels. But if you find yourself using warm-weather fuels in colder climates, there are additives designed to lower the pour point and keep diesel fuels flowing. Other than those considerations, you shouldn't have to worry about using additives in your car's fuel tank.

Fuel System Maintenance

Most people don't think a lot about fuel system maintenance. When something goes wrong with the system, they have it fixed. Until then, they put gas in the tank and hope for the best. But there are a few maintenance items that will help keep your car's fuel system in better condition, to improve gas mileage and dependability while reducing emission levels. These maintenance items fall into two main categories: filter replacement and system cleaning.

Filter Replacement

Most cars have three filters for the fuel and induction system:

- Air filter
- Fuel filter
- EVAP filter

Filters in a Car

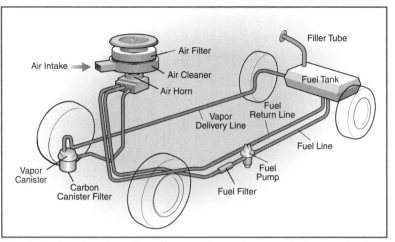

The air, fuel and canister filters have to be serviced regularly to maintain proper engine operation.

Here's what's involved with checking and replacing each one.

Air Filter — Engines have to be able to breathe. Without the necessary air, the engine can't support combustion. A clogged air filter actually chokes the engine. The air filters in today's cars are a paper or spun fiber element that captures dirt particles from the air entering the engine. When it becomes clogged, the air filter can reduce engine performance and fuel economy while increasing emission levels.

You should check the air filter at least every six months or 15,000 miles. In most cases, the repair shop will check the air filter with every oil change. To check the air filter, hold it up to a light. If you can see light through the filter, it's still clear enough to work properly. If you can't see light through most of the filter element, replace it.

You can clean the air filter between replacements by tapping it gently against a flat surface. This should dislodge any loose dirt particles from the filter element. But when in doubt about the condition of the air filter, replace it. It's a cheap way to keep the engine breathing freely.

Fuel Filter — The fuel filter strains the fuel entering the fuel system to prevent dirt particles from clogging the small passages or nozzles, or from getting into the engine. A clogged fuel filter can cause the car to hesitate, lose power or even keep it from starting at all.

What type of filter you have and how often it requires maintenance depends on the fuel system your car's engine has:

Carbureted Engines — The fuel filter for most carbureted engines is a small, inexpensive element made of paper, spun fiber or a porous metal casting.

Because of its low cost and ease of replacement, you should have the carburetor fuel filter replaced during every tune-up.

Fuel-Injected Gas Engines — The fuel filter for most fuel-injected gas engines is a large paper element, sealed in a metal container. Because of its large size, the fuel filter will work much longer without clogging than those in carbureted engines.

But these fuel filters do clog if left unattended for too long or if the fuel is exceptionally dirty. When that happens, the car will bog down, lose power and even shut off on hard acceleration. If there are no driveability problems to indicate the need for early replacement, the fuel filter on most fuel-injected cars should be replaced every 60,000 miles or so.

Diesel Engines — The fuel filter is one of the hardest-working components on a diesel engine. That's because of the quality of many diesel fuels, along with the various microbes that live in those fuels. In addition, diesel engines are highly susceptible to water contamination. That's why many diesel fuel filters also have a water separator as part of the canister.

Check your owner's manual. If your car's fuel filter has a water separator, make sure to drain it regularly. The manual should give you a time or mileage requirement for draining the separator. And have the filter changed at least every year to prevent the system from becoming fouled or clogged.

EVAP Filter — The EVAP, or evaporative system, is part of a gasoline engine's emission control system. It captures gas vapors that otherwise would evaporate into the atmosphere and returns them to the engine to be burned.

Most EVAP systems have a flat, spun fiber filter that sits under the evaporative canister. While a clogged EVAP filter won't affect performance too much, it will affect vehicle emissions, and should be checked and changed periodically. In most cases you should ask to have the EVAP filter checked or changed with every tune-up. That's often enough to keep the EVAP system working properly.

Fuel and Induction System Cleaning

A service item that's been popping up in repair shops all across the country is the *fuel and induction system cleaning* service. It involves running a cleaner through the fuel system, throttle body and intake manifold. This cleaner removes carbon and deposits from the injectors, throttle and intake, and even works its way down into the combustion chamber and catalytic converter in some cases.

Many people believe that this is just some type of scam. The fact is, it's a real service with real benefits for fuel economy, engine performance and lower emissions. In fact, it wouldn't be overstating things to call fuel system cleaning the tune-up for the new millennium. Let's start with the whys and why nots, and then we'll discuss how often you should have your car's fuel system serviced.

"I never needed my fuel system cleaned before." Not true. In fact, carburetors often were cleaned very thoroughly as part of a regular tune-up. The difference was that the carburetor was wide open, with large passages that the technician could reach from under the hood.

Most basic tune-ups included cleaning the choke, throttle plate and all of the carburetor passages using a highly caustic, aerosol cleaner. This cleaner removed the carbon and deposits from the entire carburetor and then ran through the engine, where it cleaned away deposits built up on the intake, valves and combustion chamber — much like the fuel system cleaning service does today.

What *has* changed is just how critical this cleaning service has become. That's because today's fuel systems work with clearances and tolerances that measure in microns — some less than half the thickness of a human hair. Even the smallest deposits on these components can have a dramatic effect on engine performance.

Keep in mind that today's cars must adhere to very strict fuel mileage and emissions standards. Years ago, manufacturers could overcome the effects of fuel system deposits simply by enlarging passageways and dumping more fuel through the system.

Today that isn't one of the choices: To meet the standards for fuel economy and emissions, fuel systems measure fuel more precisely than ever before. There's no room for error — or for deposits.

"OK," you say, "you've convinced me. My car's fuel system needs to be clean. But why does it have to be cleaned by a service technician? Can't I just run one of the off-the-shelf cleaners through the gas? For that matter, the gas I use claims it includes detergents to keep my car's fuel system clean — why do I need to have it cleaned at all?"

Let's start with the first question: Do you need to have your car cleaned professionally, or can you use one of the off-the-shelf cleaners? Most off-the-shelf fuel system cleaners aren't effective enough to clean the fuel system properly. In fact, in many cases those cleaners can cause more damage than they correct.

Take a look at the label. Most fuel system cleaners offered to the do-it-yourselfer market use a base of kerosene, alcohol, methanol, acetone or ketones. These are highly flammable, highly caustic cleaners, which can cause one of two specific problems:

1. The cleaner's high flammability causes it to burn up long before it can become effective in the combustion chamber. This not only reduces its effectiveness, but also can create additional deposits, compounding the original problem.

2. The caustic nature of these cleaners can damage the fine electronics, seals and coatings in many of today's injection systems.

Fuel and induction system cleaning is a service with real benefits. It can improve performance, reduce fuel consumption and lower emission levels. How often should you have your car's fuel system serviced? Most experts agree that — provided you aren't experiencing a problem — you should have your car's fuel and induction system cleaned yearly to keep it running right.

CHAPTER 7

The Cooling System: Taking the Heat

In This Chapter

• • • • • • • • • • • •

- An introduction to your car's cooling system: how it works and why it's necessary

- The different types of coolant available

- How to check coolant level and protection

- How to check the hoses

- What to do if your car's engine overheats

The word *combustion* means "to burn." Internal combustion engines create power by burning a mixture of air and fuel in the combustion chamber. This, by definition, creates heat. And when combined with the friction that takes place inside the engine, that heat can quickly become high enough to melt engine components.

To prevent that, all internal combustion engines use some type of cooling system. Most use a liquid — called *coolant* — to carry the heat away from the engine and release it to the atmosphere. Here's how: Coolant fills an area of the engine called the *water jacket*. This water jacket surrounds all of the cylinders in the engine. As the engine heats up, the heat flows from the engine components to the coolant.

The *thermostat* starts out closed, keeping the coolant from moving. This allows the engine to warm up faster. Once the coolant reaches about 200 degrees F, the thermostat opens. Now the *water pump* causes the coolant to flow from the engine and through the *radiator*.

The radiator conducts the heat through its fins, where outside air flowing past the fins carries the heat away. The now-cooler coolant continues back to the engine, where it can take on more heat and begin the cycle all over again.

Cooling systems also include a *heater core*, a small radiator that allows heat from the engine to warm the passenger compartment.

Cooling System

The cooling system allows the coolant to transfer heat from the engine to the outside air, which keeps the engine from becoming too hot.

What is Coolant?

Now that we know what coolant does, what is it? Coolant is a mixture of plain water and chemicals designed to protect the engine. Many people refer to coolant as antifreeze, but that's not quite right. Antifreeze is an outdated term, used to describe an additive that simply prevents water from freezing.

But today's coolants do much more than just prevent water from freezing. To begin with, they also increase its boiling point. A 50 percent mix of water and coolant will increase the boiling point about 15 degrees F. That extra cooling capacity is important for cars with air conditioning, which creates even more heat in the engine compartment.

Secondly, coolants protect and maintain the cooling system. They prevent rust, neutralize acids and lubricate moving parts such as the water pump. And they provide this protection for a wide variety of materials, including cast iron, steel, aluminum, copper, brass, rubber and even plastic.

And finally, today's coolants still provide protection against freezing: A 50-50 mix of a typical coolant and water will lower the freeze temperature to less than 30 degrees below zero.

Coolant Comes in Many Types

If there were only one type of coolant on the market, choosing the right one would be easy. Actually, there are four main types of coolant available today. We'll take a quick look at all four and help you choose the right one for your car.

Standard — This is the basic, ethylene glycol-based coolant that you're probably already familiar with. It'll usually be green or orange in color and will provide adequate protection for most cooling systems for two years or 30,000 miles.

Dex-Cool™ — This is a relatively new blend of ethylene glycol and special polymers, designed to provide protection for five years or 150,000 miles. But there's a catch: It only works that long if it was used originally by the manufacturer. That way, the special additives bond with the metals inside the system, creating an extra shield of protection. If used with a car that came with standard coolant, Dex-Cool™ is only good for two years or 30,000 miles.

Environmentally Friendly — The problem with ethylene glycol is that it's deadly to animals and harmful to the environment. That's why at least one manufacturer has come out with a propylene glycol-based coolant, designed to be safe for the environment. One slight problem, though: Propylene glycol won't mix with other coolants, so the system has to be drained completely to switch it over to this type of coolant.

Recycled — Another effort to protect the environment has been the introduction of recycled coolants to the market. This usually is only available through repair shops, which recycle the coolant on-site or purchase it in drums through a volume recycling company. This recycling process involves filtering the old coolant, neutralizing acids and replacing the lost additives to the coolant. Then the recycled coolant is as good as new — often for a lot less money.

So which coolant should you use in your car's cooling system? Check your owner's manual, or, in some cases, you'll find a sticker indicating the type of coolant on the radiator support. If the car came with Dex-Cool originally, stick with it to enjoy the extended maintenance schedule. If your car didn't come with Dex-Cool originally, there's really no point in switching over to it. Use a standard coolant instead.

And if you're interested in protecting the environment, you should choose either a propylene glycol coolant or find a repair shop to recycle your old coolant. Either of these choices is a good way to protect your car and your environment.

Coolants Come in Assorted Colors

You might think that since there are only four different types of coolant out there, each one would be a different color. That way it would be easy to tell which one you have in your car. Sorry, no such luck. The color has no bearing on what type of coolant it is.

The color in engine coolants is just a dye, and the coolant manufacturer can add just about whatever color dye it wants. So while the coolant in your car may be any color of the rainbow, that doesn't tell you what type of coolant it is.

Checking Coolant Level and Protection

For the coolant to work and protect the cooling system properly, it must meet three conditions:

- The system must be full.
- The concentration must be correct.
- The pH level must be balanced.

If any of these conditions is incorrect, the cooling system may not work properly, or the system may become damaged.

Most coolants are deadly if taken internally, and even the propylene glycol coolants aren't particularly good for you.

Tip Provided by
Ed Donovan
AAA Mid-Atlantic

Never open the radiator cap while the engine's hot. Relieving the pressure can cause the system to boil over and cause serious burns to you and anyone nearby. Always let the engine cool down all the way before relieving the pressure on the cooling system.

Checking the Level

The first condition — making sure the system is full — is easy. If you aren't having any problems with leaks or overheating, you can simply check the overflow tank. That's usually a little plastic tank near the radiator. It should be marked *Coolant* or *Overflow*. If you aren't sure where your car's overflow tank is, check your owner's manual.

The overflow tank usually will be translucent so you can see the level just by looking at the side of the tank. And it'll be marked with two levels: cold and hot. The cold level will be lower than the hot level, due to expansion. To check the coolant level, look at the side of the overflow tank. If the level isn't between the two lines, it's low. Add enough coolant — premixed with an equal amount of water — to bring the coolant to the appropriate level.

To do so, always make sure the engine is cold. **Never open the radiator cap when the engine is hot.** And make sure the engine is off. You don't want the system heating up while you have the radiator cap off.

Once you're sure the system is cold, open the radiator cap. Push down and turn the cap counterclockwise at the same time. The cap should click once when it's halfway open. Continue turning the cap until it's loose. Then remove the cap and check the level. If the radiator cap has a locking lever, lift the lever first, then push and turn the cap to remove it.

In a sealed system — which is any system that uses an overflow tank — the coolant should be filled to the top of the radiator neck. If it's low, add enough premixed coolant to fill the system and then wait. As the coolant bleeds down into the system, the level should continue to drop slowly. Keep adding coolant, a little at a time, until the system appears full. Then replace the radiator cap, pushing in and turning clockwise until the arrows on the cap align with the overflow hose.

Don't bother adding stop-leak to the system core to fix a leak. In general, those are just stopgap measures, and they only work with certain types of leaks. What's more, in some cases those stop-leak additives can actually clog the radiator or heater, turning a small problem into a much larger one.

Above all, make sure you take your car into the shop as soon as possible. Low coolant means the system has a leak, and should be checked and repaired as soon as possible.

Checking the Protection

The next thing you need to check with coolant is its protection level. The coolant may appear green (or blue or red) but still not provide adequate protection against freezing or overheating for the climate in your area.

The most accurate way of checking coolant protection is with a device called a *refractometer*. With just a drop or two of coolant, the refractometer shows the exact protection level of any type of coolant on the market. The problem is, a refractometer is fairly expensive — too expensive for most car owners to buy. But most shops should have one and will be happy to check your coolant protection level — often for nothing — while you're having other service work performed.

Another way to check coolant protection is with a hydrometer. The hydrometer is a small chamber with a bulb for sucking some of the coolant out and measuring its specific gravity — its density compared to plain water — which it converts to a temperature measurement.

Using a Hydrometer

Hydrometers provide a low-cost method of checking the coolant protection level. But be careful: Hydrometers aren't all that accurate, and you'll need a different one for ethylene glycol and propylene glycol coolants.

A third method of checking coolant protection is with a test strip. This is a paper strip with test chemicals on it. When you dip the strip into the coolant, the chemicals change color. Then you can match the color with a sample chart on the side of the package to determine the protection level.

While not near as accurate as a refractometer, test strips have an important advantage: They also measure coolant pH. This is a measurement of whether the coolant is too acidic or alkaline.

If the coolant pH isn't balanced, you have two options: You can flush the cooling system and replace the coolant, or you can add a bottle of antirust, designed to neutralize acids in the system. If the coolant is due for changing, that's the way to go. Have the system drained, flushed and refilled with new coolant.

But if the coolant is clean and hasn't reached its replacement time or mileage, you can add a bottle of antirust and have the coolant checked again, after the antirust has had a chance to work its way through the system. In most cases that'll bring the pH level back to normal.

Coolant antirust is a great way to extend coolant life and is a good idea to use on the "off" years when you don't change the coolant.

Changing the Coolant

A service procedure that's often overlooked or ignored is changing the engine coolant. Once called a "flush-and-fill," this service can have a dramatic effect on your car's longevity. Here's why: Coolants contain a number of additives to provide protection to the car's cooling system. These additives include acid neutralizers and lubricants for the water pump.

But over time, these additives wear out or dissipate. The pump problems caused by the loss of lubricants are obvious. But the problems caused by acids building up in the system are less so.

The acids build up slowly and usually aren't strong enough to cause serious damage by themselves. But cooling systems are made up of a number of different metals. Think back to your high school chemistry. When dissimilar metals are placed in an acid solution, the combination creates a battery.

And therein lies the problem. Batteries work through a process known as *electrolysis* — the transfer of electrons from one metal to another. This transfer actually erodes metal from one surface, causing the metal to pit, wear and eventually leak.

CAUTION

Used coolant is a hazardous waste. Never pour coolants into a drain or public sewer system. Always take waste coolants to a local repair shop to be recycled or disposed of properly.

Tip Provided by
Lou Ickes
AAA West Penn/
West Virginia/South Central Ohio

So, to keep the cooling system in good condition, it's important to keep fresh coolant — with the proper pump lubricants and acid neutralizers — in the system. That's why you should have the cooling system drained and the coolant replaced regularly.

Unless your car's cooling system has become seriously clogged and contaminated, you can ask a service shop to do a simple drain and fill to keep the system working like new.

Checking and Replacing Hoses

One of the most common failures to cooling systems is when a hose blows out. While there's no way to prevent this from happening completely, there are ways of reducing its likelihood.

To begin with, you should have the hoses replaced at least every other time you have the coolant changed; that is, every four years or 60,000 miles. That way the hoses never have the chance to deteriorate and fail.

In between those replacements, you also should check the hoses at least every few months or so. Most repair shops will check the hoses when they change the engine oil, but to be sure, ask for it. Chances are they won't even charge for checking the hoses if they're already doing something else to the car.

But you also can check the hoses yourself. It's easy to do and only requires a few minutes. Here's how:

- Make sure the engine is off and open the hood.
- Examine the hoses. Look for cracks, tears, leaks, rubbed spots, oil contamination or spots that have ballooned up. Any of these conditions indicate a worn or damaged hose that should be replaced.
- Grab onto the hoses one at a time and squeeze them in various locations. You're looking for spots that are overly soft or hard. A good hose should allow you to squeeze it, without feeling mushy.
- Check along the ends of the hoses for stains or wet spots that indicate leaks. If the hose has clamps that tighten with a screwdriver, you may be able to correct a leak by tightening the clamp.
- While you're at it, don't forget to check the coolant level. Remember, if the coolant is low, there has to be some type of leak. Engine coolant doesn't evaporate.

If everything looks OK, great. The hoses should be OK for the next few months or so. But if you find a problem, you should have the hose checked professionally and replaced.

WARNING

Keep your hands away from the fan blade, even with the engine off. On some cars the fan can start running by itself, without the engine running or the key on.

Tip Provided by
Phil Linck
AAA Missouri

TECH TIP

If you still want to replace a hose yourself, be careful. Never try to pull the hose directly off of the necks. They become "glued" into place, and you'll end up pulling the neck out of the radiator before you get the hose to come off. To make things easier, slice the end of the hose with a utility knife. Then the hose should peel right off the neck, without damaging it.

Tip Provided by
Approved Auto Repair Staff
AAA Western and Central New York

Want to replace the hoses yourself? A few years ago it would have been easy to do. But today it can be difficult to *find* all of the hoses, let alone replace them. And even if you could find them, many use special clamps that require special tools for removal. In most cases, you're better off leaving them to a professional automotive technician.

If the Engine Overheats

You can tell whether your engine is overheating one of four ways:

1. The temperature light comes on while driving.
2. The temperature gauge indicates the temperature is too high.
3. You see large amounts of steam coming from under the hood.
4. The engine suddenly begins knocking, gurgling and losing power.

If you experience any of these conditions, what you do about it depends on the condition. If you see steam coming out from under the hood, pull over as soon as it's safe and turn the engine off. Turn your flashers on and don't open the hood until the engine cools off.

But if there's no steam coming from under the hood, you may be able to force the engine to cool off. How you do that depends on whether your car has electric cooling fans or not. If your car *does* have electric cooling fans, open the hood and see if they're running. If not, or if only one of them is running, turn the air conditioning on. If the A/C turns the fans on, the engine should cool down fairly quickly. If your car doesn't have electric cooling fans, turn the heater on, full hot, high blower. If you're stuck in traffic, hold the engine speed above idle.

Regardless of which type of car you have, if the temperature light doesn't go out in a minute or two, or if the engine starts steaming, pull over and shut off the engine. Turn your flashers on and let the engine cool.

Once the engine has cooled down, open the hood and check for any signs of a leak. If a hose has a hole and it's right near one of the ends, you may be able to cut the end of the hose off and reattach what's left. Always make sure you'll have enough hose left to reach the neck before you cut the end off.

WARNING

Never attempt to check an overheating problem while the engine is hot. Always give the engine time to cool before you check it.

Tip Provided by
William J. Linsenmayer
AAA Ohio Automobile Club

If the hole is near the center of the hose, you may be able to repair it temporarily with duct tape or electrical tape. Dry the area off and wrap the tape around the hose to get a good seal. Then open the radiator cap and start the engine. With the engine running, slowly add water or coolant until the system is full or until you run out of coolant.

Then replace the radiator cap, *but only turn it to the first click.* That will prevent the system from building up pressure and should allow you to drive to the nearest repair shop for more permanent repairs.

If you can't see a problem or there's no way to fix it temporarily, your best bet is to call for emergency roadside assistance. Never try to drive the car with the engine overheated. That's a great way to destroy the engine.

CHAPTER

8

The Electrical System: The Power to Keep Things Working

In This Chapter

• • • • • • • • • • • •

- An introduction to the primary components of your car's electrical system

- How to choose a new battery

- How to determine if your car's charging system is working properly

- What to do if the charging system stops working

- What to do if your car won't start

- How to jump-start your car's battery

You might think your car runs on gasoline, but without electricity your car isn't going anywhere. Electricity provides the power to crank the engine and the spark to fire the cylinders. From the computer controls to the light that comes on when you open the door, it's all run by electricity.

The Battery

The battery is the initial source for all of the electricity in your car. In most cars, it's a 12-volt, wet-cell battery that creates electricity through an electrochemical reaction caused by immersing a series of dissimilar metal plates in an acid solution. The result is a transfer of electrons, which is another way of describing electrical current flow.

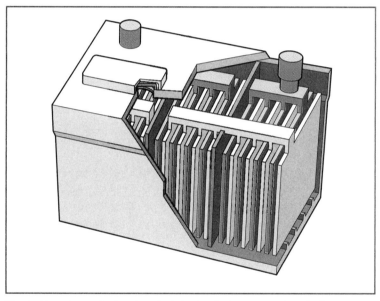

The battery is an electrochemical device that creates electrical power by immersing dissimilar metal plates in an acid solution.

Some manufacturers have begun experimenting with dry-cell battery configurations. Over the next few years, auto manufacturers will introduce 42-volt electrical systems. But in general, the processes and procedures for maintaining those systems will be similar to the 12-volt, wet-cell battery.

To keep your car firing on all cylinders, it's important to have a good working electrical system, and that begins with maintaining the battery. In general, a good working system involves three things: keeping the battery filled, charged and clean.

Maintaining the battery is easier today than ever before, because in most cases, today's batteries do not need water added under normal driving conditions or the batteries are sealed. They still have acid in them, but you can't add to it even if you wanted to. If your car's battery does have removable caps, you should check the level about once every three weeks or so to make sure it's full. Here's how:

- Make sure the engine's off.
- Open the hood.
- Remove the battery caps. (Do not force the cap off; it may appear to be removable but is not.)

Look inside each battery cell. See the little ring, near the bottom of the opening? That's the "Full" line. The battery should be filled to one-quarter of an inch below the bottom of the opening. If the water level is low, add a little distilled water to bring it up to the proper level. Then replace the caps. (Be sure to wear eye protection and be careful when you do this.) If you're adding water to a battery when the outside temperature is below freezing, ensure that the battery is charged immediately after the water is added.

But remember: Most of the time you won't have removable caps to fill the battery. Some batteries have a small "eye" that indicates whether the battery is full or not. In most cases, the eye should be green when the battery is full and charged. Some imports use yellow to indicate that it's full. If the battery eye turns black, it means the battery either is too low or it has become discharged. Take your car into the shop to have the battery charged and tested.

Next, check the battery itself. Is it clean or covered in grease and dirt? Believe it or not, grease on the battery case actually can discharge the battery. If the battery is dirty or greasy, clean it with a mild detergent and a damp cloth. Be careful: Batteries contain sulfuric acid. If you get any on your skin, always flush it off immediately with a solution of cold water and baking soda to prevent acid burns. And always wash your hands with soap and water after handling the battery.

Finally, take a look at the battery terminal ends. Those are the cable ends that connect the battery cables to the battery terminals. The terminal ends should be clean and free of any signs of corrosion.

Should You Service the Battery Yourself?

Once upon a time, not so long ago, battery service was easy, even routine. You disconnected the old battery, pulled it out of the car, dropped in the new one and – *voila!* – the battery was new. But today's cars have thrown a little something extra into the mix: electronics. Today's cars are brimming with electronics, from the digital clock on the dash to the computer that controls the engine and transmission operation.

And those computers have memories. Over time, they learn how you drive, what type of gas you use, what components have begun to wear and so on. Then they compensate for those variations to provide you with good performance. If you disconnect the battery, those memories get wiped clean, and it can take several weeks to have the computer relearn those memories. In the meantime, the car runs, but not as well as you'd like it to. And don't forget the presets such as the radio and power seats. Disconnecting the battery erases them.

Here's something you may not have thought about: Does your car radio have a theft code? Many do, and it can cause you some real grief if you disconnect the battery. The theft code works like this: If the power from the battery gets interrupted for any reason, the radio stops working. To get it working again, you have to enter the theft code. Easy enough — if you know what the code is *and* if it's something you *can* enter.

Some cars — most notably some of the upscale European cars — don't provide those codes for the car owner. If the theft code gets triggered by losing power, the only way to reset the radio is to remove it and send it back to Europe to be reset. That's why most shops use a memory saver — a little device that plugs into the electrical system and provides just enough power to keep the memories and theft codes intact. It's a good reason why, if you aren't experienced in auto repair, you should leave the battery service to a pro.

Buying a New Battery

Automotive batteries come in different types, sizes and price ranges. Whether you buy it yourself or get it through your repair shop, it's important to know how to identify the differences and how to choose the one that's right for your car.

Warranty — Most decent batteries last three to four years, regardless of warranty length. Very often manufacturers offer longer warranties at higher prices just to hook you on their batteries. If you get rid of the car before the warranty expires, they win. If the battery fails while still in warranty, you take it back and they prorate your refund from the cost of a new battery.

So if you paid $70 for a seven-year battery and it lasts only four years, they give you about $30 in credit toward a new battery. But be careful, a lot of companies offer the warranty based on the suggested retail price rather than the selling price. So, it may be to your disadvantage to have the warranty adjustment rather than simply purchasing a new one. The battery doesn't last any longer, but you're hooked into buying from them a second time. In general, a four-year to six-year warranty is plenty. The average life expectancy for a battery is about 36 - 42 months. If it fails early, you're protected, and you aren't paying for an overly optimistic warranty. Just remember to keep a copy of the warranty and receipt.

Size — Don't be fooled by the size of today's batteries. New technology has enabled battery manufacturers to develop much smaller batteries that provide just as much power as the older, larger ones did. When choosing a battery, there should be only three size considerations:

1. Does it fit properly in the battery tray?
2. Is the battery short enough for the hood to close without causing a problem?
3. Are the terminals on the proper sides, so the cables will reach?

As long as the answer to these three questions is "yes," the battery will fit just fine in your car.

Capacities — This is the real difference between batteries: how much power they provide and for how long. All battery manufacturers must declare this information using three standard measurements:

Cranking Amps — Cranking amps (CA) is the amount of power the battery provides for cranking your car's starter for 30 seconds at a temperature of 32 degrees F (zero degrees C), while maintaining at least 1.2 volts per cell (7.2 volts total). As you might expect, the higher the number, the more power the battery provides for starting your car.

Cold Cranking Amps — CCA is virtually the same as cranking amps, but with one difference: The measurement is taken at zero degrees F (−17.8 degrees C). So cold cranking amps indicates how well the battery will crank the starter in really cold weather — when the engine is hardest to crank.

Reserve Capacity — This measurement indicates how long your battery would keep the engine running if the alternator stopped charging. It's a measurement of how many minutes the battery will deliver 25 amps at 80 degrees F (27 degrees C) while maintaining at least 1.75 volts per cell, or 10.5 volts total. In other words, this is about how long your car will continue to run with the headlights, wipers and defroster on, if the alternator quits.

So what capacities would be adequate for your car? Bigger doesn't necessarily mean better when it comes to batteries. The climate where you live plays a factor. In a cold climate, bigger is better, but if you live in a hot climate, the lighter CCA may offer an increased life expectancy for the battery.

Not sure what the specifications were in the original battery? Check the owner's manual. If it doesn't provide the battery specs there, check the application guide from the battery manufacturer. They'll usually list a minimum recommendation for your car. Choosing a battery with higher specs won't hurt, but choosing a battery with lower capacities could leave you stranded one day.

Special Features — Some battery manufacturers now are offering batteries with special features above and beyond the ability to create electricity. These features may include theft protection or cold-weather heaters, to name a few. Do you need these features? Not really. But if you'd be more comfortable with them, go for it. Just remember that you're paying for those features, so it's up to you to decide if the features are worth the extra price.

The Starter

You climb behind the wheel, put the key in the ignition, turn it to start, and the engine begins to crank. The sound you hear is the starter, a large electric motor that cranks the engine in the proper speed and direction to enable the engine to start.

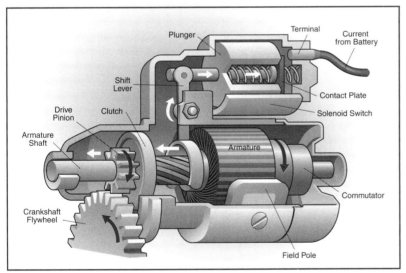

The starter is a small, powerful electric motor that spins the crankshaft when you turn the key. This gets the process of internal combustion going to start the engine.

Starters work very hard to crank an engine, and they require a lot of electrical current — far more than could go through the ignition switch. That's why starters use a *solenoid*, a type of high-current relay designed to allow the ignition switch to energize the starter without having to deliver that much current itself.

In most cases, there won't be any kind of maintenance for keeping your car's starter working. Either it'll work or it won't. One thing you can do to keep the starter working right is to release the ignition key as soon as the engine starts. And never turn the key to start while the engine is running. Either of those conditions will reduce the starter's life drastically.

The Charging System

The battery provides the voltage to run the car, but if left on its own, the battery would discharge in a matter of hours. To keep the battery fresh and fully powered, cars have a charging system. In most cases, that means an *alternator*. An alternator is a type of generating device that's been wired to produce direct current (DC). This is a little different from the alternating current (AC) you'd get from a standard generator, in that the DC from an alternator is always positive. In general, an alternator does a better job of keeping the battery charged than an old-style generator would.

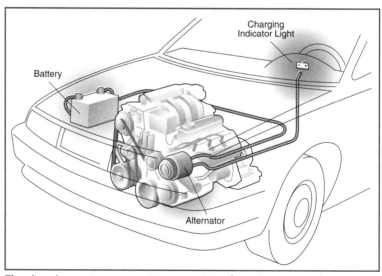

The charging system on most cars consists of an alternator, a battery, and an indicator on the dashboard to let you know if the system's working or not.

Most alternators are driven by the engine through a drive belt. In most cases, their output is controlled by the car's computer system or an electronic regulator built into the alternator. While there's no real maintenance for the alternator beyond keeping the belt tight and in good condition, you should try to keep an eye on whether it's charging properly. There are three main ways to do that:

- Dashboard indicators
- Sound
- Voltmeter

Dashboard Indicators

Let's start with the dashboard indicators. If your car has a CHARGE or BAT light, the light should come on if the system stops charging. During normal operation, the light should come on when you first turn the key on, with the engine off. It should go out when the engine starts.

The only problem is that dash lights are notoriously inaccurate. They'll often indicate the system is working fine, when it's actually not charging. So, if your car's headlights seem to dim when you come to a stop or it's cranking a little on the slow side, take it in to have the electrical system checked — even if the charging light stays off. A somewhat better dashboard indicator is the electrical gauge. These gauges may be voltmeters, amp indicators or ammeters.

Sound

Another way to check the alternator output is by its sound. When charging, an alternator whines or "sings" to you with a high-pitched, consistent sound. The louder the whine, the higher the amperage it's delivering. A problem in the alternator often is accompanied by a variation in the whine. A warble in the sound may indicate one of the circuits in the alternator isn't working. If the alternator stops singing entirely, it's probably not charging at all.

While this can be a good indicator, interpreting the sound from an alternator can take a lot of experience. The important thing to remember is that if the alternator sounds different than normal, you probably should take the car in to be checked.

Plug-In Gauges

Technicians use voltmeters and ammeters to test electrical systems all the time. While the gauges they purchase probably are too costly for you to invest in, there is a gauge you may want to consider: a cigarette lighter gauge. Several places offer an inexpensive voltmeter that plugs right into your car's cigarette lighter. Since the cigarette lighter is connected to the electrical system, it provides a good voltage sample for monitoring the system.

A voltmeter reads total system voltage. During normal operation, the voltage should be between 13.5 and 14.5 volts. If it drops below about 13 volts, the alternator is no longer charging. It's a good check and is easy to read and fairly dependable. While not an absolute necessity, this can be a good way to keep an eye on whether your car's alternator is charging, particularly if the only thing you have on the dash is a light.

If the Alternator Stops Charging

Momentary discharging may not indicate a problem at all. For example, if the light flickers on when you're idling, in gear, with the lights, defrosters, radio, turn signal and any other electrical device you can think of turned on, that's probably normal. As long as the light goes out as soon as you start moving, don't worry too much about it. Have the system checked when you get a chance, for your own peace of mind.

But if the light comes on and stays on, it indicates a real problem. If your headlights are off, you'll probably be able to drive to your repair shop. Shut off any other power accessories to keep from draining the battery.

Keep in mind that the belt that turns the alternator also may turn other accessories. If the belt breaks, it could cause you to lose the power steering or air conditioning. Or, if the belt also drives the water pump, it won't be long before the engine starts to overheat. If you see the temperature start to climb or the TEMP light come on, pull over as soon as it's safe and shut off the engine. If it's nighttime or your headlights are wired to remain on all the time, you may not make it to the shop before the battery gets too low to keep the engine running. Your best bet is to call for roadside assistance.

Starting Problems

Engine Won't Crank

1. When you turn the key, nothing happens: no dash lights, no sound, nothing. Pop the hood and check the battery. Either the battery is completely dead or there's a wiring problem in the starting system. Try jump-starting the battery. If that doesn't work, you'll probably have to call for assistance.

2. When you turn the key, you hear a rapid clicking sound, and the dash lights dim. This is a classic low-battery symptom. Jump-starting the battery should get the engine to start. Then take the car into your repair shop and explain the problem. They should charge the battery, and check the charging and starting systems. The problem could be a bad battery or alternator, or it could be something as simple as a loose alternator belt.

3. When you turn the key, the dash lights come on, but you don't hear anything when you turn the key to start. Make sure you have the shift selector all the way in park. Move it out of park and then back, or try starting it with the shifter in neutral. If your car has a manual transmission, make sure you have the clutch pressed all the way to the floor.

    If that doesn't help, you can try jump-starting the battery, but it probably won't work. There's a good chance your car has a bad starter or a problem in the starting circuit. That could mean a problem in the ignition switch, neutral safety switch or starter solenoid. Call for assistance and explain the symptoms carefully to the repair center.

4. The dash lights come on when you turn the key, then go right out — and the engine doesn't crank — when you turn the key to start. But when you release the key, the lights slowly come back on. This is another classic: the bad battery connection. When you turn the key to start, the starter pulls so much current that it breaks the connection. Then, when you release the key, the connection slowly comes back. The connection provides enough power to turn the dash lights on, but not enough to crank the starter.

    Cleaning and tightening the battery terminals may fix this problem. Or you may be able to get enough of a connection simply by twisting the terminals a little. Either way, once you get the car started, you should take it into the shop to have the cables cleaned and tightened properly, and the rest of the charging/starting system checked.

5. When you turn the key, you hear a single, hard clunk. Turn the headlights on and try again. Do the lights dim slightly when you turn the key? If so, you probably either have a bad starter or a seized engine. Regardless of which, you'll have to call a tow truck to come and get your car.

One thing you could try is to tap on the side of the starter with a hammer while someone else turns the key. This sometimes works if the starter is bad, but don't count on it.

If the headlights don't dim at all, or just barely dim, there may be a connection problem between the starter solenoid and the starter itself. But you'll probably still have to call for a tow truck and have your car taken to your local repair shop.

6. When you turn the key, you hear a loud, scraping or grinding noise, like metal on metal. This is another classic complaint. Either the starter drive is bad, the ring gear on the flywheel damaged or both. The only difference from your standpoint is cost. Both of them require having the car towed and repaired.

    You may get the starter to engage if you try turning the key a couple times, but let go of the key right away if you hear the noise again. If the car *does* start, don't press your luck. Take it right over to your local repair shop and have the problem fixed.

Engine Cranks but Won't Start

1. The engine seems to crank normally, but the engine doesn't even sound like it's *trying* to start. Is there gas in the tank? Are you sure? Gas gauges are notoriously inaccurate. If you have to move your head to one side to get the needle to move off empty, try adding some gas to the tank.

    When you first turn the key on, do you hear the fuel pump run? In cars with electronic fuel injection, you should hear a light hum for a few seconds from around the fuel tank. That's the electric fuel pump running.

    If you don't hear the fuel pump run for a couple seconds when you first turn the key on, try cranking the engine until the oil light goes out. That may start the pump running and allow the engine to start. Make sure you let your repair shop know what you had to do to get the engine to start.

2. The engine cranks normally, and it sounds like it wants to start but just won't catch. You may have flooded the engine. Hold the gas to the floor and try again. (Let the gas pedal up when it finally starts.) If it's raining out, the ignition system may be wet. A service technician may be able to dry the system out using compressed air. Or you can wait until it dries out on its own. Either way, you'll probably need a new set of plug wires, a coil, or a cap and rotor (depending on what type of ignition system your car has).

3. The engine cranks really unevenly, in a repetitive-sounding pattern. Sounds like you may have a bad timing chain or timing belt. Don't waste your time trying to start it any longer: It isn't going to happen. And if by some miracle it *does* start, you'll probably get stuck a few blocks away. Call a tow truck and have it towed to the repair shop.

Engine Starts but Shuts Off

1. The engine starts right up, but shuts off as soon as you release the key. This is the classic symptom of a bad ignition switch. When you release the key, the ignition switch shuts the power off to the ignition system. A new switch should fix it. Don't try to keep it running by holding the key to the start position. That'll just destroy the starter and possibly the flywheel, and turn a relatively inexpensive job into a costly proposition.

2. The engine starts and runs, but when you put the transmission in gear, the car lurches and the engine shuts off. The converter clutch in the transmission torque converter probably is engaging when it shouldn't. On some cars you can bypass this by disconnecting the torque converter clutch solenoid; but unless you know which wire to pull, forget about it. Call for assistance and make sure you explain the symptoms completely, in case the problem goes away temporarily during the tow to the shop.

3. The engine starts and runs, but seems to idle slowly and stalls when you come to a stop. This probably is a fast idle problem. When the engine is cold, it's supposed to idle a little faster than normal to keep the engine running. You may be able to drive using two feet until the engine warms up: one on the gas to hold the idle up a little and the other for the brake. But don't keep driving it this way. Take your car to your repair shop, explain the problem and describe what you had to do to overcome it. They should know what to do from there.

How to Jump-Start the Battery

If your car's battery is dead, you may be able to get started by giving it a jump — connecting another battery to yours using jumper cables and letting the good battery provide the extra current needed to crank the starter. Once your car's engine starts, the alternator should provide the power necessary to keep it running until you can get to your repair shop.

Here's how to jump-start your car's battery:

Step

1   Pull the "live" car close enough to reach between the batteries with jumper cables.

2   Turn off the engine.

3   Open the hoods.

4   Identify the positive and negative terminals on each battery. Look for the (+) and (−) symbols.

5   Connect one red clamp from your jumper cables to the positive (+) terminal on the dead battery.

6   Connect the other red clamp to the positive (+) terminal on the live battery.

7   Connect one black clamp to the negative (−) terminal on the live battery.

How to Jump-Start a Battery

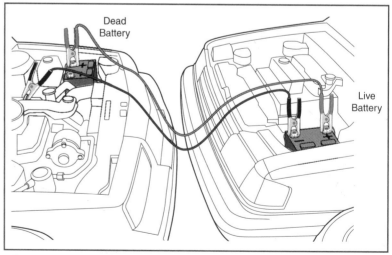

When jump-starting a battery, always connect positive to positive, negative to negative.

Before jump-starting the battery, follow these tips for your own safety and your car's protection:

- Always wear protective gloves and glasses or goggles.
- Never attempt to jump-start a battery that's frozen, cracked, gassing excessively (vapors or smoke escaping from the vents) or damaged.
- Make sure both cars involved have similar electrical systems. Never try to jump-start a battery using a car with a different electrical system. Some older cars have 6-volt systems; a newer one may have a 42-volt system.
- Never smoke or allow any type of flame or spark near a battery. The hydrogen gas from the battery is highly explosive.
- Always maintain proper polarity when connecting a battery: positive to positive, negative to negative.

Tip Provided by
Thomas Rich
AAA Wisconsin

This procedure presumes both cars are wired "negative ground." Virtually every car built during the last 50 years is negative ground, so it's a good bet yours is, too. But some older, more exotic cars are positive ground. If you suspect your car is positive ground, call a professional to jump-start your car.

8 Connect the other black clamp to a good ground on the engine block away from any moving parts. Make sure you get a good connection. Attempt to start the car with the dead battery. If it doesn't start, quickly go to the next step.

9 Start the engine on the live car and allow the battery in your car to charge for a few minutes.

10 Attempt to start your car. If the engine was flooded, you may have to hold the gas pedal all the way down to clear the flood.

11 Once the car starts, leave it running. Disconnect the jumper cables in reverse order, being careful not to touch the clamps to each other or to anything else on the cars.

After you get the engine started, keep it running and have someone follow you to your local repair shop. Explain the problem and have them check the charging/starting system. This involves checking the battery and cables, the starter and the charging system. You may need a new battery or just need to recharge the old battery.

CHAPTER

9

Drivetrain Maintenance: Keeping Your Car Moving

In This Chapter

• • • • • • • • • • • •

- An introduction to clutches, transmissions and differentials: what they are and why they're necessary

- Seven steps to make your car's clutch last longer

- Different types of automatic transmission fluid

- How to check the ATF level and condition

- How to deal with a transmission problem

Your car's drivetrain takes the horsepower from the engine and turns it into torque to turn the wheels. When we talk about the drivetrain, we're really discussing two main components: the transmission and the differential. But it also includes lesser components that connect them to the wheels, such as the driveshaft, axles, U-joints, CV-joints and, on cars with manual transmissions, the clutch.

Of course, there are a lot of variations on these components. For example, most rear-wheel drive cars and trucks use a separate transmission and differential, connected by a drive shaft. On the other hand, most front-wheel drive cars have a transaxle, which combines the transmission and differential in one case.

What's more, the transmissions themselves come in a variety of flavors. There's the standard, or manual transmission, which requires a clutch to connect it to the engine. Then there's the more common automatic transmission, which connects to the engine through a torque converter. Finally, there's a newer type of transmission that appears on some Subaru and Hondas: a CVT, or continuously variable transmission. Even the differentials come in two main types: standard and limited slip, sometimes called positraction.

In this chapter, we'll take a look at the drivetrain components and discuss what you should know about service procedures to keep your car's drivetrain working like new.

Power vs. Speed

You're driving down the on-ramp, preparing to merge with traffic on a major roadway. What you need now is power — enough power to get from 15 to 55 fast. You watch for your opening, step down on the throttle, and you feel the surge of power as your neck snaps back.

You might not have realized it, but that power you felt had more to do with the gear ratio than the engine's power. That's because the gear ratio determines *torque*, a measure of the power the wheels apply to the roadway to get your car moving.

When you first stepped down on the gas pedal, your car's transmission downshifted into first gear. That lowered the *gear ratio* between the engine and the wheels, creating the surge of power you felt.

Basically, gear ratio is the difference in size between two gears. For example, in low gear, the drive gear — the gear connected to the engine — is very small. The driven gear — the gear connected to the wheels — is very large. This difference in gear size allows the engine crankshaft to turn more times than the wheels, which provides more torque at lower speeds.

Low Gear

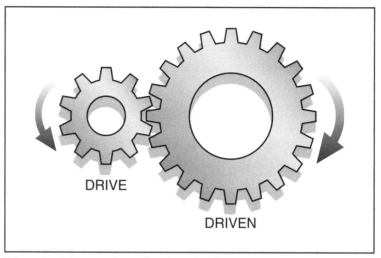

When the drive gear is smaller than the driven gear, the combination develops high torque at low speed. This is how the transmission develops low gear ranges.

Once you get moving, you want more speed while requiring less power. Shifting to a higher gear range reduces the difference in size between the gears. The crankshaft still turns faster than the wheels, but the difference isn't as great.

Eventually you reach *direct drive*. This is where the two gears are the same size, and the crankshaft turns the same speed as the transmission output shaft. In direct drive, many transmissions skip the gearing and allow the crankshaft to mesh directly with the output shaft.

Direct Drive

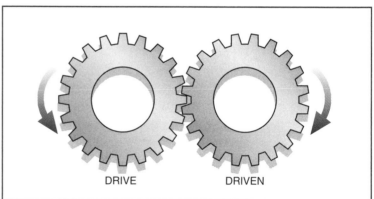

When the gears are the same size, the ratio between them is 1-to-1. This is direct drive, and in most transmissions the gears are eliminated and the input and output shaft mesh directly.

Most newer transmissions offer something beyond direct drive: *over-drive*. This is where the drive gear is larger than the driven gear. In overdrive, the output shaft actually turns faster than the engine crankshaft to create higher speeds while providing less power. This helps increase overall gas mileage and reduces emissions.

Overdrive

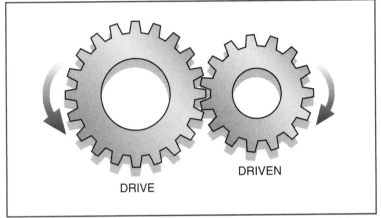

Overdrive is when the drive gear is larger than the driven gear. This combination produces a ratio that's less than 1-to-1, causing higher speeds at lower torque.

This is the primary function of every transmission on the road: to provide power transfer at a wide range of gears for the different speeds and loads required.

Manual vs. Automatic

The name says it all. Manual transmissions are the ones that *you* shift from one gear to the next. Automatics shift themselves, based on a series of engine load and vehicle speed signals. All you do is put them in drive.

The transmission is a series of gears, meshed to provide a path for the power to travel. By moving the shifter, a slider in the transmission moves. The slider locks one of the gear sets to the output shaft, providing a specific path for power flow. Each gear set provides a different gear ratio, so by shifting through the gears, you can choose which gear range suits the driving conditions.

A Manual Transmission

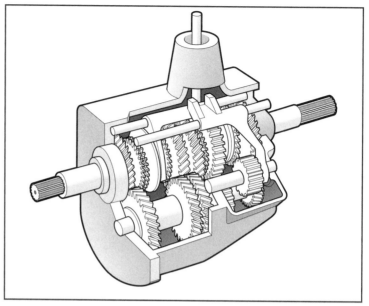

A manual transmission is a series of gears meshed together. Shifting gears actually locks one of the gear sets to the output shaft, creating the path for the desired gear ratio.

Automatic transmissions also provide different gearing, but they use oil pressure to apply individual *clutch packs* or *bands* inside the transmission to create the various gear ranges. By applying a clutch pack or band, the clutches grab onto one of the gear train components, which either holds or turns that component. The combination of holding and turning enables the gear set to create different gear ratios within the transmission.

An Automatic Transmission

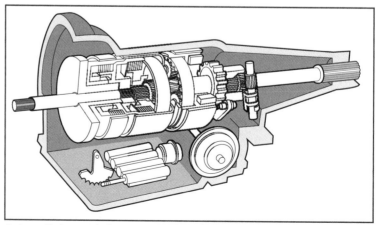

Automatic transmissions use a series of clutch packs and bands to lock various geartrain components together to create the various gear ranges.

What really makes the automatic transmission different is that it shifts automatically. By measuring engine load and road speed electronically, a computer system controls transmission operation. The computer decides when the transmission should shift and then delivers an electrical signal to create that shift. The transmission still uses oil pressure to control the clutches, but now the computer regulates which clutches apply and when.

Another difference between automatic and manual transmissions is how they transfer power from the engine. Manual transmissions use a clutch; automatics use a fluid coupling called a *torque converter*.

A torque converter is an oil-filled device that uses oil flow to transfer power. An *impeller* mounted to the crankshaft slings the oil into a *turbine*, which is connected to the transmission input shaft. This oil movement transfers the motion from the crankshaft to the input shaft without the two being connected mechanically. That's why you can come to a complete stop in a car with an automatic transmission, without having to press a clutch pedal. There's no mechanical connection that has to separate.

Once the oil gets through the turbine, it's redirected through another set of fins called a *stator*. The stator prevents the "used" oil from dragging against the torque converter, so it increases the torque converter's efficiency.

Torque Converter

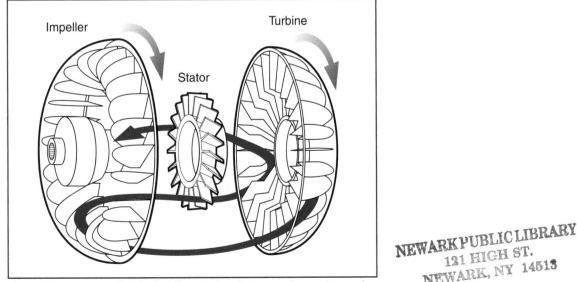

The torque converter is a hydraulic coupling between the engine and transmission. This is what allows the car to come to a full stop without stalling the engine or having to press a clutch pedal.

While very efficient, there is some power loss through the torque converter. What's more, during normal operation, torque converters create a lot of heat. To eliminate that heat and pick up a little extra efficiency, most manufacturers now add a torque converter clutch to the converter. This clutch applies once the car is cruising down the road to create a direct mechanical connection between the engine and transmission, eliminating the slip and reducing operating temperatures.

While most cars use one of these types of transmissions, there are a few less-common types. Some early vehicles used semi-automatic transmissions, which still required manual shifting but didn't have a clutch pedal. Some of these transmissions were based on a manual transmission, using vacuum and electric controls to operate the clutch. Others were closer to automatics, but without the governor to force the shift automatically.

The CVT, or continuously variable transmission, uses a special belt that runs between two pulleys to transmit power between the engine and the wheels. As the power and speed requirements change, the pulleys change in width, which alters how deeply the belt rides in them. This changes the effective radius of the pulley, which varies the "gear ratio."

Some of the new electric or hybrid gas/electric cars don't use any transmission at all. The primary motor on these cars is electric, and it operates under a much wider range of speeds, so a transmission isn't necessary.

Service Procedures: Manual Transmission

Manual transmissions really only require one type of maintenance: having the fluid level checked. But to do so, you usually have to have the car on a lift, so it isn't a job for the average car owner. In general, you should have the fluid checked whenever you have your engine oil changed. Most repair shops will do this automatically, but it won't hurt to ask for it when you drop the car off.

There are only two common reasons to change the manual transmission oil. One is if it becomes contaminated, usually with water. In that case, the problem that allowed the water in will need to be corrected and the fluid replaced. Another reason to change the oil in a manual transmission is if there's a problem such as hard shifting or grinding gears. In some cases, this type of problem can be corrected by replacing the transmission oil with a different type or a different weight oil. Both of these situations are rare, so, in general, you shouldn't have to worry about changing the fluid in a manual transmission.

Service Procedures: Clutches

Clutch Assembly

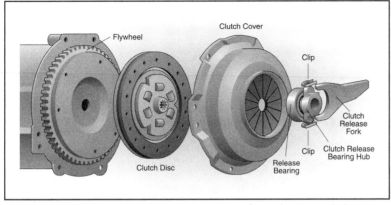

The clutch engages and disengages the engine from the transmission on cars with a manual transmission.

Clutches are a normal wear item; that is, they're designed to wear and eventually will wear out. You can increase the life of your car's clutch by keeping it in good working order.

Start by finding out how your car's clutch pedal operates. Some use a cable, others a linkage. Still others use a hydraulic control system, much like the system used to apply the brakes. Your owner's manual may offer some information on this. If not, check with your repair shop. They'll be able to tell you how your car's clutch operates.

If your car uses a clutch cable or linkage, it may need to be lubricated now and then. Ask to have it lubricated when you take your car in for an oil change. If the clutch is controlled hydraulically, the system will need the fluid level checked. Some manufacturers may recommend changing the clutch fluid. Check your owner's manual to be sure and follow its recommendations.

All clutches require some level of freeplay; that is, free movement that occurs before the release mechanism actually contacts the clutch. Some clutches are self-adjusting, designed to keep the right amount of freeplay automatically. But some of them will require you to lift up on the clutch pedal to allow the pedal to reset. The owner's manual will tell you whether you have to lift the pedal occasionally to allow the clutch to self-adjust.

Whether your clutch is self-adjusting or not, you should check the freeplay once in awhile. Too little freeplay will allow the clutch to slip; too much will keep it from releasing all the way when you press the pedal. Both conditions will wear the clutch prematurely.

To check clutch freeplay:

- Make sure the engine is off and the car is parked for this test.
- Press slowly on the clutch pedal, using one finger.
- Pay attention to how far the pedal moves before you feel additional resistance. That movement is the freeplay.

Most clutches should have between three-quarters of an inch and 1.5 inches of freeplay. If the freeplay seems too high or too low, take your car in to your local repair shop to have it checked professionally. If the freeplay is wrong, they should be able to adjust it. If it's OK, they can show you what to look for when you check it yourself.

To Check for a Slipping Clutch

A slipping clutch means the clutch isn't grabbing all the way. At first it may be just an annoyance, but eventually the clutch will stop grabbing enough to move the car, and you'll end up walking. If you suspect your car's clutch is slipping, start by checking for freeplay. If you don't feel any freeplay at all, take your car in immediately to have the clutch checked. A simple adjustment may fix the problem, while driving without freeplay will quickly destroy your clutch.

But if there's plenty of freeplay, there's another way to check for a slipping clutch that will indicate a problem long before it gets that bad. Here's how:

- Find an open roadway, without too much traffic.
- Start driving down the road and shift into high gear as quickly as possible. Try to get into high at about 20 to 25 mph.
- Once you're in high gear, press down on the throttle.

If the clutch is OK, the engine should bog down. But if the engine revs up freely without the car moving any faster, plan on having the clutch replaced.

Seven Easy Steps to Make Your Clutch Last Longer

1 Make sure your clutch is adjusted properly. Never drive a car with a misadjusted clutch.

2 Always press the clutch all the way to the floor to release it. Never hold the clutch halfway to the floor, and never drag the clutch while standing at a stoplight.

3 When starting out, always release the clutch smoothly while applying just enough gas to get moving. Never "pop" the clutch or allow the clutch to drag for longer than necessary.

4 Always release the throttle when shifting between gears. Never hold the throttle down during a shift.

5 Always remove your foot completely from the clutch while driving. Never rest your foot on the clutch pedal.

6 Always use your brakes to stop the car. Don't downshift to slow it down, unless emergency conditions require it.

7 Don't shift more often than necessary. Feel free to skip a gear (shift from first to third or second to fourth) if you can do so without putting a lot of strain on the engine or drivetrain.

If you follow these seven simple steps, your clutch should last a good long time.

Automatic Transmission Fluids

Automatic transmission fluid, or ATF, does much more than just lubricate moving parts. It helps hold the clutches and bands to their mating components, cools the transmission and even provides the connection between the engine and the transmission to drive the car, and it lubricates many parts.

For the transmission to operate properly, the fluid must be full, clean and the right type. That should be easy — and once upon a time, it was. But these days there are all kinds of things to consider, beginning with what type of oil your transmission uses.

Dexron is still around and is used in lots of transmissions. It's been upgraded several times. The latest version is Dexron III, which works in anything that calls for Dexron ATF. Dexron is used in GM transmissions, as well as many imports.

Ford has its own ATF, called Mercon. Its specifications are basically identical to Dexron, so most transmission fluids you see on the shelves will be identified as Dexron III/Mercon. That means they're fine for use in transmissions that call for either type of ATF.

IMPORTANT

A number of manufacturers have started eliminating the transmission dipstick, effectively "sealing" the transmission. Their feeling is that transmission leaks are less likely than the problems caused by car owners adding the wrong fluid to their transmissions.

If you can't find the transmission dipstick on your car, or the owner's manual tells you there isn't one, you may have to take your car to a repair shop to have the transmission fluid level checked.

This may involve using a special "test dipstick" or a special procedure for checking the fluid level. Either way, you probably won't be able to do it yourself.

Once you've found the transmission dipstick, the procedure for checking the ATF level is fairly standard.

With all the different types of ATF on the market, how can you be sure which type yours takes? Read the owner's manual. It specifies the exact type of fluid necessary for your car's automatic transmission.

If you need to add a quart, use the type recommended in your car's owner's manual.

One last point about ATF: There is a difference between brands. Low-priced, no-name brands may lack some of the friction modifiers and additives so important for the proper operation of your car's transmission. To avoid transmission problems, always use a quality, name-brand ATF.

Checking the Fluid Level

With all the functions performed by automatic transmission fluids, it's pretty obvious that nothing's more important for proper transmission operation than maintaining the proper fluid level. To check the transmission fluid in your car, start by finding the transmission dipstick. On rear-wheel-drive cars, the transmission dipstick usually will be at the back of the engine, toward the passenger side of the car. On front-wheel drive cars, the possibilities are endless.

One thing that will help you identify the transmission dipstick is the size of the tube. The transmission dipstick tube usually is three-quarters of an inch or so in diameter — much larger than the engine oil tube, since the tube also is where you add ATF. But if you can't find the transmission dipstick, refer to your owner's manual.

Here are the steps to follow to check the level of the transmission fluid.

Step

1 Start the engine.

2 Move the shifter slowly through the gears, one at a time. Wait for the transmission to engage before moving to the next gear.

3 Once you've gone through each gear, move the shifter back to park.

4 Set the parking brake, if you haven't already done so.

5 Open the hood.

6 Remove the transmission dipstick and wipe it off.

7 Examine the dipstick for the full mark and whether there are separate marks for cold and hot levels.

8 Slide the dipstick all the way down into the transmission, then pull it back out and check the level.

9 If the fluid is low, add a little, then shift through all the gears again before rechecking the level. Keep doing this until the level is correct for the present operating temperature.

10 Once the transmission is full, reinstall the dipstick. Make sure it's seated all the way onto the tube.

Transmission Dipstick

Be sure to check the transmission fluid at the correct temperature. On some transmissions, the fluid level goes up as the transmission heats up. On others, it goes down.

Checking the ATF Condition

While you have the dipstick pulled out of the transmission to check the fluid level, there's something else you should check: the condition of the transmission fluid. There's a lot you can tell about a transmission by the condition of its fluid.

WARNING

Be careful reaching into the engine compartment with the engine running. Avoid moving components and make sure you aren't wearing any loose clothing that can become entangled and pull you in.

Tip Provided by
James P. Kerr
Automobile Club of Hartford

TECH TIP

On most transmissions, the fluid level tends to rise as the transmission warms up. You may have as much as a quart difference showing on the stick. But on some units, particularly GM front-wheel drive transaxles, the fluid level goes down when it reaches normal operating temperature.

Tip Provided by
Martin W. Koonce
New Jersey Automobile Club

CAUTION

Never overfill the transmission. If the level is too high, the fluid will foam and cause driveability and durability problems. It could even blow out the vent, leak onto the exhaust and catch fire.

Tip Provided by
John Kozak
AAA East Penn

TECH TIP Some front-wheel drive transaxles have a separate fluid collection pan, or sump, for the differential, which contains a different type of oil and must be checked separately. But checking the differential fluid usually involves putting the car on a lift and removing a side plug — too involved a job for the average car owner. Ask your repair shop whether your car's transaxle has a separate pan and make sure they check the level during every oil change.

Tip Provided by
Ed Gouker
AAA Southern Pennsylvania

By condition, we're talking about a combination of color and odor. Look at the fluid on the dipstick and then give it a sniff. Clean fluid is transparent and almost odorless. Burnt fluid can be opaque, and it gives off a strong odor, indicating a problem in the transmission.

As we look at the different possibilities for the condition of the ATF, we'll assume that your transmission fluid started out red. That's the color most transmission fluids are. But remember, there are other colors for ATF, and the original color will affect how it looks later, after it's been in use for a while.

Red or Slightly Brownish with no Discernable Odor — This is how the fluid should look and smell. Based on this, there's nothing obviously wrong with the transmission. Plan on having the fluid changed at the normal maintenance interval.

Brown with a Slightly Burnt Odor — The fluid's burnt. If the transmission is working properly, you should have it serviced now rather than wait for the maintenance interval. If you have it serviced now, there's still a chance the transmission will be OK.

Dark Brown or Black with a Strong Burnt Odor That Knocks You Off Your Feet — The transmission probably is ruined and will have to be rebuilt. Don't expect a fluid change to help at this point. While the transmission is being rebuilt, make sure they flush the cooler and check it for proper flow.

Milky Color Like a Strawberry Milkshake — There's water in the transmission, usually from a leak in the cooler. The source of the water will have to be repaired first, and then the transmission will have to be rebuilt. Even if the transmission works OK now, the water will work its way into the clutches, rusting the backing and lifting the clutch material away.

Small Metallic Flakes Like Glitter in the Fluid — A metal component inside the transmission is wearing or damaged — either a bushing, thrust washer or metal hard part. In any case, the transmission probably will have to be dissassembled, checked and repaired.

Service Procedures: Automatic Transmissions

One of the best ways to keep your transmission in good working order is to have it serviced regularly. This usually involves these basic steps:

Step

1 Drain the oil.

2 Clean the fluid collection pan, or sump.

3 Replace the filter or screen.

4 Adjust bands and linkages (some units only).

5 Reinstall the fluid collection pan with a new gasket.

6 Replace the fluid with new ATF.

At the same time, the technician can examine any debris in the pan to determine whether it indicates a problem that would require additional work. It's not uncommon to find large quantities of clutch material in the bottom of the pan, even if the transmission seems to be working OK.

Assuming the debris in the pan doesn't indicate a major problem, cleaning it out is a good way to keep the transmission working longer. And replacing the fluid removes acids, varnish and oxidation, while replenishing worn-out friction modifiers.

The best service involves removing the pan, examining its contents, cleaning it, replacing the filter and reinstalling the pan, just like on the older service procedure. Then it's followed by a complete fluid change, using a machine to pump out the rest of the fluid.

Don't forget: A transmission service is just a maintenance item. It won't repair a transmission that's already damaged or worn out. But performed regularly, transmission services can help keep your transmission in good working order for years longer than one that wasn't serviced.

Extending Transmission Life

Having a transmission rebuilt can be an expensive, daunting proposition. Not only does it cost more than most other repairs, but in most cases you have to depend on the skill and honesty of a specialty shop instead of your regular repair shop. Maybe that's why the average car owner is more concerned about transmission repairs than anything else on a car.

It's also why there are so many items designed to fix your transmission problems, without having to remove it from the car. Not just the basic "rebuild in a bottle" additive. There also are *devices* available such as auxiliary coolers and inline filters that are designed to keep your transmission in the best of health.

But do they really work? Some do, some don't. Let's start with the additives. These additives claim to be able to free sticking valves, and soften and swell seals. Unfortunately, by the time you notice a problem, loose valves and swollen seals won't help a bit. In general, you'd do better by having the transmission serviced — *before* a problem occurs.

Does that mean all additives are useless? No, there are a few out there that work really well for neutralizing acids, improving the fluid's resistance to heat and replacing friction modifiers. But they're usually only available to the professional market, and you won't find them in the average chain store. So, if your repair shop recommends an additive to help keep your transmission in good shape, there's a good chance it's a worthwhile investment.

What about auxiliary coolers and inline filters? Are they worth the investment? Once again, the answer is "maybe," but this time it depends on the transmission and how you drive it. Let's start with the coolers.

Heat is the No. 1 cause of automatic transmission failures. Transmission temperatures can easily exceed 350 degrees F (177 degrees C). That's hot, and that heat can quickly turn your car's transmission into ashes. The factory cooler helps, but if you place any additional strain on your car's transmission, a cooler can be a good investment.

Who should consider an auxiliary cooler? Anyone who:

- Tows a trailer
- Travels through mountains
- Drives through deserts or extremely hot climates
- Does excessive stop-and-go driving

What about inline filters? Inline filters mount in the cooler lines to provide additional filtration for the ATF. In most cases, they're a great investment. But there is an exception: some ZF transmissions with lock-up converters.

ZF is a German transmission that appears in some of the upscale imports, such as Audi, BMW, Jaguar, Porsche, Range Rover, Rolls Royce, Saab, as well as some VWs, Fords and Chryslers.

The problem is, when the converter clutch applies, the flow through the cooler reverses on some ZF transmissions. If you put an inline filter in the cooler line on one of these units, every time the converter clutch applied, all of the dirt in the filter would flush back into the transmission.

As long as your car doesn't have a ZF transmission with a lockup converter, an inline filter is a great, inexpensive way to keep your transmission working right.

Why a Differential?

Differentials have three main functions. To begin with, they lower the overall drivetrain gear ratio, usually somewhere between 2-to-1 and 3-to-1. This allows the transmission to operate in and around direct drive and reduces the load on the transmission.

Secondly, many differentials rotate the power flow by 90 degrees. That's because most rear-wheel drive cars have *lateral* transmissions — transmissions that run down the length of the car. The power flow leaving the transmission is going the wrong way. The differential uses a ring-and-pinion gear set to turn the power flow 90 degrees so the drivetrain can drive the car properly.

But one of the most important functions of a differential is to allow the two drive wheels to turn at different speeds. That difference is necessary for turning corners. Here's why: When you're driving straight down the road, the wheels on both sides of the car are traveling the same distance, so they turn at the same speed. But that changes when you turn a corner.

Think of it this way: When a car turns, the wheels form an arc, or part of a circle. Because of that, the inner wheel — the wheel on the side closer to the center of the "circle" — doesn't travel as far as the wheel on the outside of the turn. To make up this difference, the outer wheel has to turn faster than the inner wheel.

If the drive wheels were locked together directly, the tires would skip or slide across the roadway when you made a turn. That's where the differential comes in. The differential connects the two wheels through four gears: two side gears and two spider gears. These gears transmit power to the wheels, while allowing them to rotate at different speeds when necessary.

But the differential, while necessary, can cause another problem. Imagine a situation where one drive wheel is sitting on dry roadway, while the other is on a patch of ice. Since both drive wheels can turn at different speeds, the differential will allow the wheel sitting on ice to spin, while the one on dry road just sits there.

To combat this condition, some manufacturers offered a *limited slip* differential. Limited slip means there can be only so much difference between the speeds of the wheels on either side of the car. There's plenty of slip for going around a turn, but a limited slip differential won't allow one wheel to spin while the other just sits there.

However, limited slip is an option on most cars and trucks. So, if you drive in areas where ice and snow are likely, consider this option when buying a vehicle.

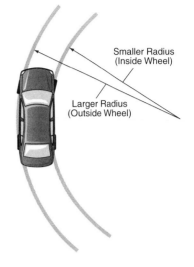

Smaller Radius (Inside Wheel)

Larger Radius (Outside Wheel)

During a turn, the outer wheels drive farther than the inner wheels. This is an important function of the differential, which allows the drive wheels to turn at different speeds.

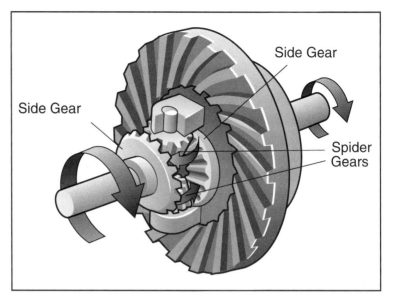

The side and spider gears allow the axles to turn at different speeds, while continuing to drive the wheels. But they can also allow one wheel to spin, preventing the car from moving at all.

Differential Service Procedures

If your car has a standard differential, the only service procedure necessary is to have the fluid level checked regularly. Since this involves raising the car and removing a side plug, it's probably best left to the repair shop. Unless it becomes contaminated, there's no reason to ever change the oil in a standard differential. As long as the level is OK, it's fine. In general, you should have the differential fluid level checked when you have the oil changed. Most shops will do that automatically, but it won't hurt to ask for it.

If your car has front-wheel drive, the differential probably is part of the transaxle. In most cases, the transmission and differential will share a common fluid collection pan, commonly known as a sump, so if the transmission fluid level is OK, the differential fluid level is, too.

Limited-slip differentials *do* require service beyond simply checking the fluid level. If your car has a limited slip differential, the fluid will have to be changed on occasion. Forgetting to service the differential could cause it to skip and make loud groaning noises on turns.

What's important about this is the fluid used. The wrong fluid in a limited-slip differential also will cause it to skip and groan on turns. So if your differential starts making noise right after being serviced, take it back to the repair shop and ask them to make sure they used the right type of fluid.

Dealing with Transmission Problems

You go out one morning, start your car, drop it into gear, and . . . nothing. The engine speed doesn't drop off, but there's no movement at all. Before you assume you need a new transmission, there are a few simple checks you can make and symptoms you can evaluate to see whether your transmission is dead or if you may be able get away with a simple service. In some cases, we'll split them up into manual vs. automatic transmission.

1. You put it in gear, and the car won't move in any range, forward or backward.

   Automatic: Check the fluid level. It could be that low. If the fluid level is OK and it still won't move in any range, you're probably looking at major transmission repairs. But there's always a possibility that the linkage has become disconnected.

   Manual: Does the clutch pedal have any freeplay? If not, it may just be an adjustment problem. But there's a good chance you're due for a new clutch.

2. The vehicle moves fine in reverse, but not forward.

   Automatic: Try putting the shifter in manual low. If it moves forward now, you probably have a bad one-way clutch in the transmission. That means the transmission has to come apart — that's the bad news. The good news is you may be able to drive the car to the shop by shifting it manually, from manual low, to second and then into drive or overdrive. That's because the one-way clutch usually only affects transmission operation in first gear, and only when the shifter is in drive. Once you get past first, the rest of the transmission will work OK.

   Manual: Try putting the transmission in third gear. In most transmissions, third gear is direct drive, so it bypasses a lot of the gearing. If the transmission moves in third, you'll probably need to have it rebuilt, but you'll be able to drive it to the shop in third instead of having to wait for a tow.

3. The transmission slips severely. If it's an automatic, it may make a whining or whirring noise.

   Automatic: You may have a clogged transmission filter. Servicing the transmission may take care of the problem, as long as you do it right away.

   Manual: If the clutch doesn't have any freeplay, an adjustment may help. If it does have freeplay, plan on a new clutch.

4. The car drives fine and then slowly loses the ability to move forward. But if you shut the key off and wait for 5 minutes, the car seems to work fine again for a little while.

   Automatic only: This is a classic clogged-filter scenario. Servicing the transmission may be all that's necessary, assuming it isn't clogged with debris from the transmission falling apart.

CHAPTER

10

Suspension and Steering

In This Chapter

- An introduction to typical suspension and steering systems and components
- How to maintain your car's suspension and steering system
- How often you should have the car's front end aligned

If roads were completely straight and totally flat, there'd be no need for a suspension or steering system. The ride would be smooth, and you'd never have a reason to turn. Whether it's a smooth, straight road or a hairpin turn, the suspension and steering systems provide the comfort and control you expect from your car.

The suspension system is a series of levers, pivots and cushions that connects the wheels to the car's frame. It's there to absorb roadway irregularities, while holding the wheels in the proper position. The steering system consists of a set of gears, linkages and pivots to keep the wheels facing the same way, while allowing you to choose which direction the car goes.

Together, the suspension and steering systems enable you to steer the car in the direction you choose at a reasonable level of comfort, regardless of the roadway surface. In this chapter, we'll look at the suspension and steering systems to see how they operate and learn what you can do to keep them working properly.

Two Types of Front Suspension

In the most general terms, there are two types of front suspension in today's cars: twin A-frame and MacPherson strut. We'll start by looking at the twin A-frame suspension, and we'll discuss some of the variations between these systems.

Twin A-Frame Suspension

The twin A-frame suspension consists of two triangular metal brackets shaped like the capital letter "A." The two feet of the letter A are the pivots that mount to the car's frame. They usually have a large rubber bushing on each end.

On the free end — the end that mounts to the wheel side of the suspension — there's a special pivot called a *ball joint*. The ball joint allows the suspension to pivot up and down, while also allowing it to rotate freely for steering. Both the upper and lower ball joint connect to a spindle, which connects the two A-frames while providing a mounting for the wheel and its bearings.

This configuration allows the suspension to move up and down while holding the wheel vertical at all positions.

The suspension uses a spring to hold the frame off the ground. This is one of the main variations between these suspension systems. The spring may be a coil-type spring or a torsion bar, and it may be mounted between the frame and the lower A-frame, or the body and the upper A-frame. There

Twin A-Frame Suspension

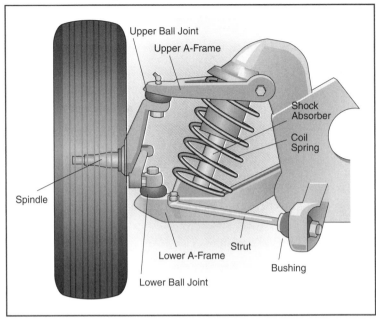

For years, the most common type of suspension was the twin A-frame style, which allowed the wheels to operate on all planes, while maintaining proper steering geometry.

Typical Shock Absorber

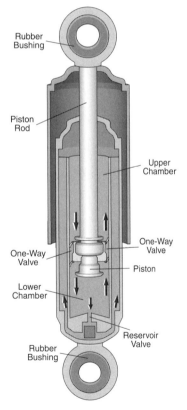

To cushion the car's bounce, manufacturers add a shock absorber to the suspension. This is a hydraulic piston that uses valves to slow the bounce and cushion the shock from the roadway.

are even some cars that use an air bag system instead of a spring to provide an even smoother ride. Regardless of position or the type of spring used, it's there for one reason: to hold the car's chassis up to soften irregularities in the roadway.

But even that isn't enough. If you were to hit a bump while driving a car with this type of suspension, the car would bounce — and continue to bounce, again and again. It quickly would become difficult to hold the car on the road. To eliminate the bounce and improve handling, auto manufacturers add a *shock absorber*.

A shock absorber is a hydraulic device, with a large piston and cylinder inside. Hydraulic fluid is channeled through a series of small openings to cushion and reduce the bounce. This helps improve the car's ride and handling.

MacPherson Strut Suspension

When front-wheel drive started showing up in the early '80s, a new type of suspension came with it: MacPherson strut. A simpler suspension system, the MacPherson strut combines the spindle, spring and shock absorber into a single, unitized component.

Locations of Different Springs

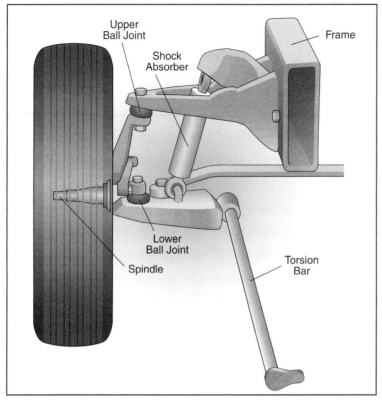

The one major difference between A-frame suspension systems is spring location. Some had a coil spring on the lower A-frame; others held the spring on the upper A-frame. And some used a torsion bar instead of a coil spring.

The bottom of the strut mounts to a control arm. The control arm has a bushing mounting it to the frame and a ball joint that connects it to the strut. The top of the MacPherson strut bolts to the inner fender and has a bearing cap to allow the entire strut to rotate.

Once again, there are variations in the MacPherson strut design from one car to the next. Some are repairable, allowing a shock absorber cartridge to be installed in the strut. Others can only be replaced as an assembly. But, in general, all MacPherson struts work the same way.

Rear Suspension Systems

The rear suspension on most cars is slightly simpler than the front suspension. It still has to hold the car up and reduce shock and bounce. And on some cars it still has to hold the wheel straight under all conditions. But on most cars, it doesn't have to steer the car, so it doesn't have to allow the wheels to pivot.

MacPherson Strut Suspension

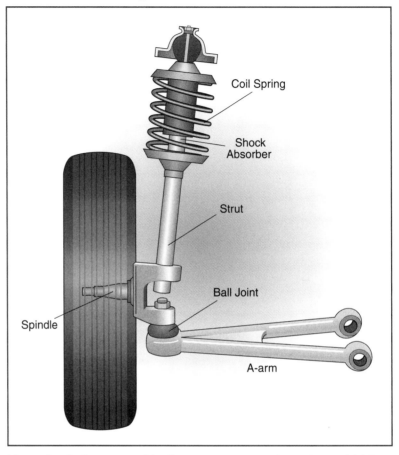

Many of today's cars use a MacPherson strut suspension system, which is lighter, cheaper and easier to adapt to front-wheel drive than other types of suspension.

There are a few rear suspensions designed to help steer the car into tight spaces. On those cars, the rear wheels actually help with the steering at slow speeds. This reduces the turning radius and makes it easier to negotiate tight parking spaces.

In general, rear suspensions are simpler than front suspensions. Probably the simplest type is the leaf spring design. This consists of an arched, flat spring assembly mounted to the frame on either end. The axle mounts to the center of the spring, and a shock absorber runs between the axle and the frame.

Another fairly simple rear suspension is the control arm suspension: Two control arms mount between the frame and the rear axle, with bushings on either end to allow them to pivot. A spring and a shock absorber mount between the axle and the frame.

Many of today's newer cars now use a modified MacPherson strut suspension. It's almost identical to the MacPherson strut used in the front, but since it doesn't have to allow the car to steer, the rear strut doesn't use a ball joint or a bearing at the top.

There also are other different types of suspensions in use, variations on these systems, and other more unusual and complex setups. These are just some of the more common ones in use today.

Two Types of Steering

You're driving down the road, and you come to an intersection. A little gas, a twist of the wheel, and suddenly you're driving in a whole different direction. Ever wonder how that turn of the steering wheel translates into the wheels turning on the ground? The answer involves gears, linkages, pivots, angles and geometry. Just like the front suspension, there are dozens of variations of steering systems. In general, they narrow into two basic systems: steering box and linkage, and rack and pinion.

Steering Box and Linkage

The steering box actually is a housing for a set of gears. A worm gear connects to the end of the steering column, and it meshes with a spur gear that faces 90 degrees away from the steering column.

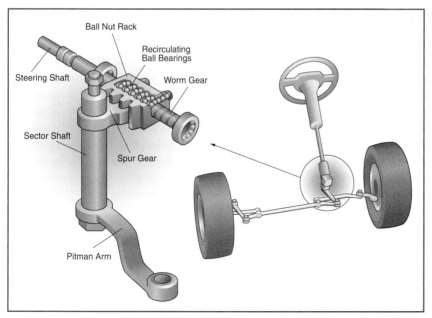

The typical steering box uses gears to convert the side-to-side motion of the steering wheel into the control necessary to turn the front wheels.

Steering Gear and Linkages

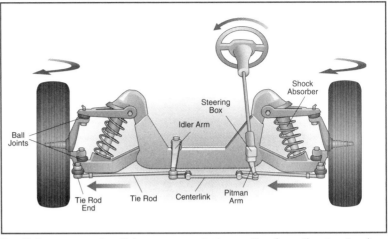

Parallelogram steering linkages transmit the motion from the steering box to the individual wheels.

The Toe Out on Turns

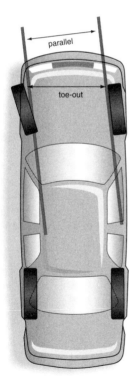

Since the inner and outer wheels track differently on turns, it's important that the inner front wheel turn more than the outer wheel. This is known as toe out on turns.

When you turn the steering, the worm gear rotates. A worm gear is like a screw, so rotating the worm gear allows it to "thread" its way into the spur gear. But the worm gear can't move: It's locked in place by the steering box. So, instead, it pulls or pushes against the spur gear, causing it to rotate.

It is this rotation of the spur gear that creates the side-to-side movement that turns the front wheels. The spur gear connects to the steering linkage through a *sector shaft*, which moves the *pitman arm* from side to side. The pitman arm connects to the steering linkage, dragging the steering linkage in the direction you turned the wheel.

The steering linkage often is called *parallelogram steering*, because the linkage forms a parallelogram. This shape enables the front wheels to turn different amounts. Here's why that's important: When you turn the car, the inner wheel follows a much tighter circle than the outer wheel. Because of that, the inner wheel must turn more than the outer wheel. The wheels actually **toe** out slightly. This feature is called *toe out on turns*. By toeing out slightly when you turn the wheel, the inner wheel turns a tighter arc than the outer wheel, so it can follow the proper track.

Rack and Pinion

The steering box system works well and has been around for years, but it tends to be a bit on the sloppy side, requiring you to turn the steering wheel a fairly large amount to turn the wheels. Most newer cars, and some older, sportier cars, use a more responsive type of steering: rack and pinion. These systems tend to be tighter, requiring only a small amount of movement at the steering wheel to turn the wheels all the way.

Rack-and-Pinion Steering

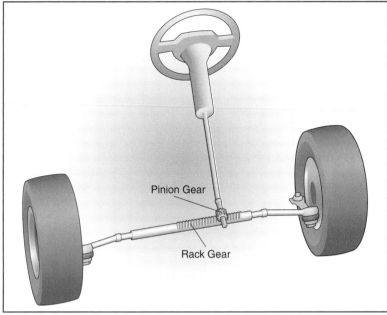

Many cars use rack-and-pinion steering, which is more responsive than traditional parallelogram steering systems.

Rack-and-pinion steering consists of a small pinion gear at the end of the steering column. This gear meshes with a flat rack gear. Turning the pinion gear pulls the rack side to side. The rack connects directly with the steering linkage to pull the steering side to side with it.

Power Steering

Most cars today offer some type of power steering. It doesn't matter whether your car has a steering box or rack and pinion. Both systems are available in a power steering version.

Power steering actually is power-assisted steering. The system uses hydraulic pressure to help push the wheels in the direction you turn the steering wheel. Turning the steering opens a valve, which directs pressurized fluid behind a piston in the steering. The pressure helps push the gear in the direction you're turning the wheel. On most cars with power steering, that hydraulic pressure comes from a steering pump mounted to the front of the engine. A belt drives the pump, which creates the pressure necessary to help turn the wheels.

Maintaining the Suspension and Steering

Today's suspension and steering systems are relatively dependable and trouble-free. But there are a few things you should do to keep them in good working order:

- Lubrication
- Repack the wheel bearings
- Check the power steering fluid level
- Regular inspection
- Alignment

In most cases, you'll only want to check the power steering fluid yourself. The other services usually require a lift and other equipment and are more suited to being done at a repair shop.

Power Steering Fluid

The power steering fluid is a hydraulic fluid the system uses to make steering easier. If the fluid is low, it will cause a growling noise that gets louder when you turn the steering. If it gets too low, the steering may become difficult.

To check the power steering fluid level:

- Make sure the engine is off.
- Locate the power steering pump. It'll usually be mounted to the front of the engine and will be belt-driven. If you can't find it, refer to your owner's manual.
- Open the pump lid or remove the dipstick. Most pumps will have a dipstick mounted to the underside of the lid.
- Wipe the dipstick off, dip it back into the pump and remove it again.
- Check the fluid level on the dipstick.

Checking Power Steering Fluid Level

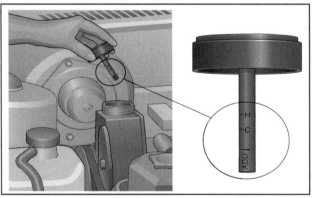

Low power steering fluid can cause a whirring noise on turns and can affect steering. So it's important to check the power steering fluid regularly.

If the fluid is low, you'll have to add some. Most auto parts stores carry power steering fluid, or you can use automatic transmission fluid. Be careful not to overfill the pump. If the fluid level gets too high, it could push out the top when you turn the wheel hard and spray all over the engine.

Once you have the level set properly, reinstall the cap or dipstick. That's all there is to checking the power steering fluid.

Lubrication

This is the "lube" part of the "lube, oil and filter" that you're supposed to have done at least four times a year. It involves pumping fresh grease into the ball joints, tie-rod ends and other rotating components in the steering and suspension system. Failure to have the suspension and steering lubed regularly can cause the components to wear and eventually fail.

Some cars have sealed suspension and steering systems from the factory. These systems usually have small plugs installed where the grease fittings normally go. If your car has plugs instead of grease fittings, have your repair shop install the grease fittings so they can lubricate the suspension and steering properly.

TECH TIP Power steering fluid doesn't get used up under normal conditions. If your car needs fluid, it indicates a leak in the system. If you have to add power steering fluid regularly, or add a lot of fluid, have the system checked for a leak.

Repacking the Wheel Bearings

Wheel bearings are ball or roller bearings that hold the wheels straight on the axle while allowing them to rotate. On drive axles, those bearings usually are either lubricated by the axle oil or are sealed components and won't require service unless they fail.

But on most non-drive wheels, the wheel bearings will need to be repacked occasionally. Repacking the bearings means removing and inspecting them, forcing, or packing, new bearing grease in between the bearings and races, replacing the seal and adjusting the bearing tension. The bearings that usually need to be repacked are the front-wheel bearings on rear-wheel drive cars and the rear-wheel bearings on front-wheel drive cars.

On front-wheel drive cars, the rear-wheel bearings don't get exposed to a lot of heat or load. In general, you should be able to get away with repacking them when the brakes get replaced. But on rear-wheel drive cars, the front-wheel bearings take quite a beating. The additional heat from the front brakes, combined with the extra load caused by turning the wheels, really puts a lot of stress on the wheel bearings.

Front Wheel Bearings on a Rear-Wheel-Drive Car

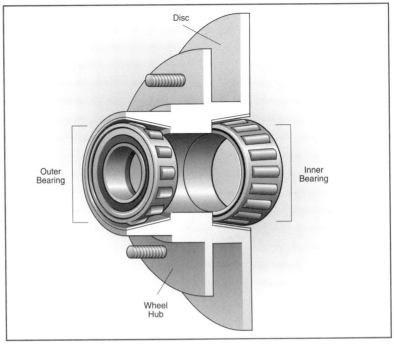

The front wheel bearings support the wheels and maintain their direction while allowing them to rotate freely. To keep them in good shape, you should have the front wheel bearing repacked regularly on most rear-wheel drive cars.

For those cars, you should have the wheel bearings repacked at least once a year. A good time to consider having the wheel bearings repacked is just before you go on vacation. That way you know your car's wheel bearings are in good shape and have plenty of grease before you go on your trip.

Inspection

Most state inspection programs include a suspension and steering check. This involves checking the ball joints, tie-rod ends and other components for looseness or wear, and a visual examination of any bushings and other components. And it usually includes a bounce check for the shock absorbers or struts.

If your state requires this type of inspection, great. In most cases, that should be all you need to make sure your car's suspension and steering are in good working order. But if your state doesn't have a safety inspection program, or it doesn't include this level of inspection, you should take your car in and have it checked at least once a year. A good time to do this is right before vacation, to make sure your car's suspension and steering will handle the additional miles without leaving you stranded.

Wheel Alignment

A few years ago, this was called "front-end alignment." But today, an alignment involves much more than just the front end. On most cars, an alignment means aligning the rear wheels with the centerline of the car and then aligning the front wheels to the rear wheels. This brings the whole car into alignment to provide additional tire life and better handling characteristics.

Depending on the shop you use, this type of alignment will carry names like *thrust angle alignment*, or *four-wheel alignment*. In general, these terms mean the same thing: aligning all four wheels to the center line of the car.

Caster

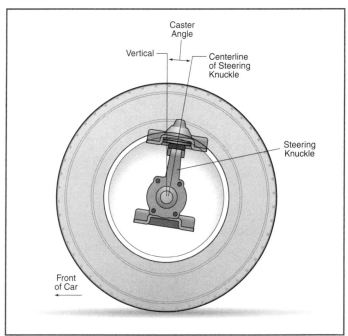

The caster is a wheel alignment specification that can be adjusted to ensure the tires drive in a straight line.

Camber

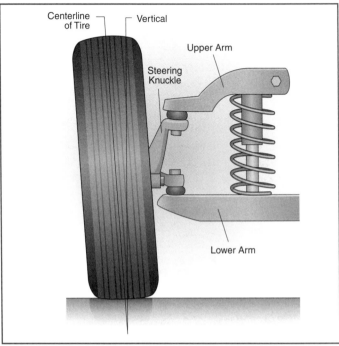

The camber is a wheel alignment specification that also can be adjusted. It checks the tilt of the tire, as viewed when standing in front and looking at the top of the tire.

Toe Out

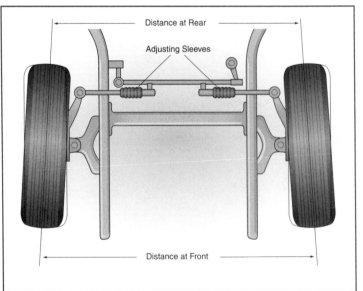

Toe is another wheel alignment specification that can be adjusted. It ensures proper steering and tire wear. This view from the front of the car shows the tires pointing slightly outward.

How often should you have your car's alignment checked? To begin with, you should have it checked if you notice any of these conditions:

- Unusual tire wear
- A pull or drift to one side — that doesn't mean you should take your hands off the steering wheel. Different levels of road crown will cause that type of drift. But if you feel the steering pulling one way or the other, have the alignment checked.
- You hit a severe pothole or curb, and the steering feels different than it did before

Remember to explain the reason you want the alignment checked so the repair shop knows what to look for. In addition, you should have the alignment checked when you get new tires. This is just an insurance policy to help make sure you get the most miles out of your new tires.

Most manufacturers also recommend you get your wheels aligned at least once a year. This isn't a bad idea and will help keep your tires in good shape. However, it isn't necessarily a cost-effective consideration. If you do decide to have your wheels aligned yearly, a good time to do so is right before your vacation, so your car will handle properly during the miles you'll be driving.

CHAPTER

11

Tires and Wheels: Contacting the Road

In This Chapter

• • • • • • • • • • • •

- How to read the tire sidewall information

- What the tire size code means

- How to compare tires, based on the Uniform Tire Quality Grading ratings

- How to choose the tires that are right for your driving characteristics

- How to maintain your car's tires

- The safe way to change a flat tire

A lot of people believe brakes control stopping, the steering controls direction, and shocks control the ride. But that's not exactly right. The brakes stop the wheels, but even when you apply the brakes, the car wants to continue moving. To stop the car, the tires have to grip the road to provide enough traction to slow the car. If the tires won't hold the roadway, they'll just skid along, and the car will keep on moving in the same direction it was traveling.

The same is true of the steering. You can turn the wheel, but without the tires to grip the road, the car would just start skidding sideways instead of turning properly.

Shock absorbers dampen the impact of bumps in the road. But between the suspension and the road, your car rides on a cushion of air in the tires. It is that cushion that smoothes out most of the small bumps and imperfections in the road. So your tires are critical for proper braking and steering — they smooth the ride, and they provide the traction to turn power from the engine and drivetrain into momentum. No wonder it's so important to have a good set of tires.

In this chapter, we'll look at your car's tires. You'll learn the different types of tires out there, how to read and evaluate the information printed on the tire, and how to maintain your tires to get the longest life out of them. You'll also learn how to compare tires and how to choose the right set for your car.

A Radial Tire

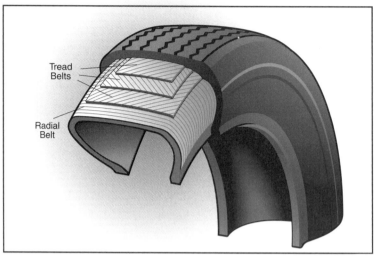

The radial direction of the tire's body belts is what gives radial tires better handling and longer mileage characteristics.

Types, Sizes and More

Today, virtually all tires are steel-belted radials. By "radial," we mean the construction of the tire — the direction the belts face. Radial tire belts line up around the outside of the tire perpendicular to the tread. This design allows the belts to flex, holding the tread against the road more evenly on turns.

The steel belt is a protective device, designed to help prevent punctures. And while it doesn't completely eliminate the possibility, it does reduce the number of flat tires that occur, as anyone who drove a car back before the days of steel-belted radials can attest.

Of course, just because the only tires available any more are radials, that doesn't mean you don't have anything to think about when buying tires. You still have several other considerations:

- What kind of tread design should you look for?
- Should you pay the higher price for a longer tread wear warranty?
- Should you pay extra for a road hazard warranty?

The list goes on and on: standard height vs. low profile, whitewall vs. raised letters, run-flat features. You name it, they've got it. And let's not forget that tires aren't all the same size. You still have to know what size tire your car needs. The good news is there's a lot of information right on the sidewall of the tire.

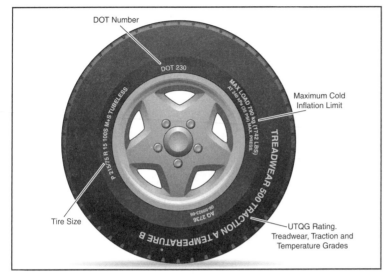

The information printed on the sidewall of the tire tells you the tire's size, construction and overall quality.

Reading the Sidewall

Walk into any tire store and look around: tires of all different styles and prices and each one claiming to be terrific. So, out of all those terrific tires, how do you choose the one that's right for your car and your style of driving? Wouldn't it be great if one tire was marked: "Hey, over here. I'm the right tire for you."

What if we said they *are* marked that way, because each tire is stamped with all sorts of information about size, tread wear, heat resistance and more. It's all there, right on the sidewall. The trick is learning how to read that information. There are four main areas on the tire that provide most of the useful information:

1. Tire size
2. Uniform tire quality grading (UTQG)
3. DOT number
4. Load, pressure and construction

We'll look at each of these areas and see what each one indicates about the tire. Then we'll cover additional information used to designate tires rated for use in the snow.

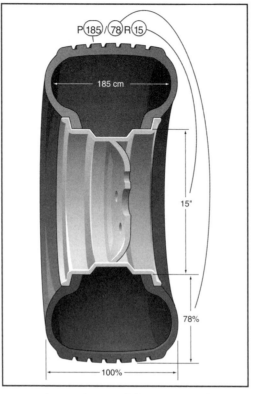

Here's what each part of the size identification number relates to the tire.

Tire Size

The size of a tire is indicated as the large set of letters and numbers near the center of the sidewall. For example: **P185/78R15 89S.** This is the size designation of the tire. The P tells you that this tire was engineered to U.S. Tire and Rim Association standards. If there's no letter in front of the size, it was engineered to European Tire and Rim Technical Organization standards. Here's what each part of the size designation means:

P — Passenger tire. If this tire were made for a light truck, it would say LT.

185 — The width of the tire in millimeters at its widest point.

78 — The ratio of the tire's height in relation to the width. This tire's height is 78 percent of its width.

R — R stands for radial; D is diagonal; B is belted. Virtually everything on the road today is a radial.

15 — This is the diameter of the wheel, measured in inches.

89S — The number is the load rating; the letter is the speed rating.

Maximum Load Capacity per Tire					
Load Index	Pounds	Kilograms	Load Index	Pounds	Kilograms
71	761	345	99	1,709	775
72	783	355	100	1,764	800
73	805	365	101	1,819	825
74	827	375	102	1,874	850
75	853	387	103	1,929	875
76	882	400	104	1,984	900
77	908	412	105	2,039	925
78	937	425	106	2,094	950
79	963	437	107	2,149	975
80	992	450	108	2,205	1,000
81	1,019	462	109	2,271	1,030
82	1,047	475	110	2,337	1,060
83	1,074	487	111	2,409	1,095
84	1,102	500	112	2,484	1,129
85	1,135	515	113	2,561	1,164
86	1,168	530	114	2,640	1,200
87	1,201	545	115	2,721	1,237
88	1,235	560	116	2,806	1,275
89	1,279	580	117	2,892	1,315
90	1,323	600	118	2,982	1,355
91	1,356	615	119	3,074	1,397
92	1,389	630	120	3,169	1,440
93	1,433	650	121	3,267	1,485
94	1,477	670	122	3,368	1,531
95	1,521	690	123	3,472	1,578
96	1,565	710	124	3,580	1,627
97	1,609	730	125	3,690	1,677
98	1,653	750			

Speed Rating	
Rating Letter	Maximum Speed (mph)
Q	99
S	112
T	118
U	124
H	130
V	149
W	168
Y	186
Z	above 149

Uniform Tire Quality Grading

These are three separate ratings for relative tire tread wear, traction and temperature. While none of these ratings lists a specific quantity, the numbers indicate ratings relative to other tires.

UTQG Rating

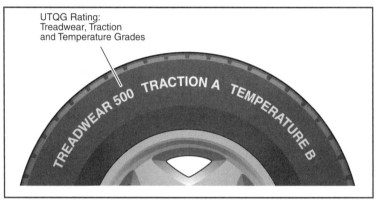

The UTQG ratings provide comparison data on the tires treadwear, traction and temperature resistance.

Here's how to read each UTQG rating:

Tread Wear — A numeric value, based on results from a 7,200-mile wear test performed on a standard course. The rating is a relative number. A tire rated 300 should last twice as long as a tire with a 150 rating.

Traction — Based on a 40 mph, straight-ahead braking test on a wet test track, this rating indicates the tire's straight-ahead braking capability. Ratings are A, B or C, with A being the best.

Temperature — Indicates the tire's ability to resist generating heat and dissipating heat under controlled conditions. Ratings are A, B or C, with A being the best. The C rating is the minimum standard required by law.

DOT Number

Every tire approved for use in the United States must carry the Department of Transportation approval, indicated by the letters DOT near the rim. The numbers following the DOT are the tire serial number. The last three digits of the serial number are the date code indicating when the tire was constructed. The first two digits are the week, and the last digit is the year. So a tire with the last three digits 230 would have been constructed in the 23rd week (second week in June) in the year 2000.

Load, Pressure and Construction

Around the rim area you'll find the maximum load rating, maximum pressure and construction description for the tire.

Special Design

Elsewhere on the tire sidewall you may find an M&S or M+S rating. This stands for mud and snow. It indicates that the tire will provide the additional traction for use in mud or snow-covered roads. If the tire says all-season, it indicates the tire is suitable for use in winter conditions, but will provide a smoother ride and better fuel mileage than a regular snow tire. The Rubber Manufacturers Association has established a set of voluntary standards for tires designed for use in severe snow conditions. These tires will carry the RMA mountain-and-snowflake logo.

Buying New Tires

The easy part of buying new tires is figuring out what size tire your car needs. Most cars have a sticker, either on the driver's doorjamb or the glove compartment door. It provides a list of the acceptable tire sizes for your car and the proper inflation to keep them. Refer to that sticker when purchasing new tires and when you check your tire pressures. If you don't see the stickers, or they've been damaged or removed, check your owner's manual for the tire recommendation.

From there, the tires you choose depends on two basic considerations: where you normally drive and the type of driving you do.

We'll start with the first one: where you normally drive. This is mostly an issue of the climate in your area. For example, if you live in the mid-Atlantic region, you probably see some snow — usually less than half a dozen days a year. In that case, an all-season tire would be a good choice.

On the other hand, if you usually drive through the south-central states, you're less likely to see snow, while temperatures tend to be higher overall. A standard tread tire with an "A" temperature rating will stand up to the heat, while providing better gas mileage than most all-season tires.

If you live in the upper Midwest or New England states, you probably could use either a standard or all-season tire during the warmer months. But in the winter you'd do better by switching to a snow tire on the drive wheels, rated for severe snow conditions. You could even consider studded snow tires with small metal pins that stick out of the tread to dig into hard-packed snow and ice and provide additional traction, if they're legal in your area.

But if you live in the southern regions near the coast where heavy rains are more of a consideration than snow, you probably should plan on buying one of the tires designed specifically to channel water away from the tread. These tires provide better traction on wet roads, while still offering great handling and gas mileage characteristics.

RMA Severe Snow Conditions Rated

This logo tells you the tire has been rated to operate under severe snow conditions.

The next consideration is the type of driving you do. This includes whether you drive in the city or on the highway, and how many miles you drive per year. If you put a lot of highway miles on your odometer — say over 30,000 a year — you're going to want a tire that lasts. You want a tire with a high tread wear rating and long mileage warranty — 60,000 miles or more. And you also may want to consider a standard tread tire, even if it means switching to snow tires in the winter. The additional gas saved probably will pay for the inconvenience of changing to snow tires and back again.

On the other hand, if you only put a few thousand miles on every year, don't overbuy. A 40,000-mile tire will last just fine. And the few dollars you would save on gas by switching snow tires on and off probably won't pay for the cost of changing the tires twice a year.

What about run-flat technology? Do you get a lot of flat tires? If not, why pay more for something so unlikely? Then again, if it makes you feel safer, maybe it's worth the extra price. That's a personal consideration for you to decide.

Should you buy a road hazard warranty? That depends on whether the roads are really beat up in your neck of the woods. If so, you may find a road hazard warranty to be a good investment. Check the price. If the road hazard warranty is just a few dollars, it could be worthwhile. But if it's $10 or $12 a tire, common sense says no.

One, Two or Four Tires?

So you check your tires and find at least one is worn beyond its useful life. How many should you buy? Do you just replace the one? Do you buy a pair? Or should you go all the way and buy a complete set? How you answer that depends on a few things.

To begin with, what do the other tires look like? If one's worn out, chances are the others are getting worn, too. If all of the tires are under about $4/32$ of an inch, this would be a good time to consider a full set of tires. Chances are you'll only get a few thousand miles out of the others, and then you'll be back, buying the rest of the set anyway.

Talk to the shop manager. He may give you a few dollars in trade for your old tires if there's still some tread left. They'll sell them to used car dealers or someone without any money who just needs to get his car on the road again. And then again, maybe they won't. Either way, you probably should spring for four tires.

But if two of the tires are better than half there, there's no reason to lose all that mileage. In most cases, you can just buy a new pair of tires. The important thing about that is to keep the new tires on one axle, either the front or the rear. Never mix new and older tires on the same axle. It could cause steering or handling problems.

The one time you might want to consider buying a single tire is if the rest of your tires are nearly new — ⁹⁄₃₂ of an inch or better. For example, if one of the tires became damaged after only a few thousand miles. In that case, it's OK to buy one tire. But try to buy the same type of tire — same brand and tread design.

Tire Balancing

While driving down the road, tires spin very fast. In some cases, they can spin as quickly as 1,000 revolutions per minute. At that speed, the centrifugal force is fairly extreme. Even the slightest imbalance will cause a vibration or shimmy that you'll feel while driving. And that vibration can cause the tire to wear, creating lumps on the tire.

If you feel a vibration that comes in around 40-60 mph, it's probably due to an imbalance. Pay attention to whether you feel the vibration in the steering wheel or through your feet. A vibration in the steering wheel usually is due to a front tire out of balance. You'll usually feel a rear tire imbalance in your feet or from under the seat.

When should you have the tires balanced? Conventional wisdom says twice a year, or every 6,000 miles. We'll talk more about that later under tire maintenance. But you definitely should have your tires balanced when they're first mounted on the wheels and if you experience a problem such as a high-speed vibration or tire wear. Remember to explain the *problem* to the shop. Let them decide whether it's due to an imbalance.

Maintaining Your Car's Tires

Your car's tires are critical for your safety and expensive to replace, so there should be no question that you want to get as much life out of them as possible. The key to that is maintenance. There are three issues to maintaining your car's tires:

- Pressure
- Rotation
- Balance and alignment

We'll look at each of these maintenance items individually. You'll learn the right way to handle each procedure and when they should be performed.

TECH TIP Mixing tires with significantly different amounts of wear can cause problems on some cars. For example, cars with antilock brakes may set a code and the ABS light may come on and prevent ABS operation if the tires turn at different speeds. And some four-wheel-drive cars may lock the drivetrain completely if the tires aren't all the same size.

Tip Provided by
Thomas Butz
AAA Central Penn
Automobile Club

Tire Pressure

One of the most overlooked maintenance items on today's cars is tire pressure. Proper tire pressure improves tire life, handling and ride characteristics, and fuel economy. In most cases, you should check the tire pressure at least once a month.

Checking tire pressure is easy. All you need is a tire gauge, available wherever they sell auto parts or supplies. They come in a number of different designs, from the simple pencil gauge to a digital electronic model. Is any one better than the others? Not really.

The real trick is finding an accurate gauge. Ask one of the technicians at the shop where you take your car to check your gauge against the one they use. As long as yours is reasonably close to theirs and provides the same reading consistently, it's dependable enough to use.

Always check the tire pressures cold. The best time usually is first thing in the morning after the car has been sitting overnight. Even sunlight will affect tire pressure, so later in the day the pressure may be altered by the heat.

To check the tire pressure, remove the cap from the tire stem and then press the tire gauge against the end of the stem. You should hear the air escape from the tire momentarily as you press the gauge onto the stem and then it should seal. If the air continues hissing while you have the gauge applied, remove the gauge and try again.

Checking the Tire Pressure

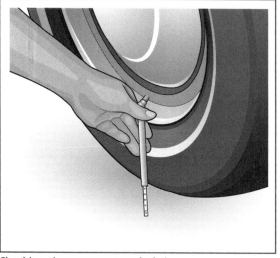

Checking tire pressure regularly is an easy way to
help your tires last longer and improve gas mileage.

Once you get the gauge to seal properly, remove it and check the reading on the end of the gauge. The reading should be equal to the factory recommendation that appears in your owner's manual, or on the sticker on the doorjamb or glove compartment door.

If the pressure is high, let a little air out of the tire and recheck the pressure. Repeat that process until the pressure is correct. If the pressure is low, add air to the tire. Chances are you won't have compressed air available, so you'll have to take your car to a gas station. The problem is, the pressure will increase as you drive there, so you won't get the right reading. Here's what you do:

- Check the pressure in each of the tires and write those pressures down.

- Subtract the pressure you recorded from the factory specifications. That's how much air you should add to each tire.

- Drive to the gas station.

- Recheck the tire pressures one at a time. Now add the amount of air you calculated in the second step.

Most gauges today read in both PSI (pounds per square inch) and kPa (kilopascals). Make sure you're comparing the right measurement to the specifications — usually that'll be PSI.

Tip Provided by
Carroll Rolf
AAA Nebraska

For example, if the air pressure in the left-front tire was 20 PSI and the specification was 32 PSI, you'd need to add 12 PSI to bring it into specs. During the drive to the gas station, the pressure may increase to 23 PSI. Add 12 PSI to that and bring the tire to 35 PSI. That should bring the tire up to the proper level. To be sure, check the pressures again the following morning.

Tire Rotation

How a tire wears depends on a number of conditions, not the least of those is which corner of the car they're on. For example, tires in the front tend to wear more on the edges than the rear tires, because front tires turn when you turn the steering wheel. That puts additional wear on the edges of the tires.

Don't forget to reinstall the caps on the tire stems. They help prevent air from leaking past the valve to keep your tire pressures where they belong.

The right-side tire may receive additional stress, because the right side of the car is more likely to make contact with potholes and curbs. Meanwhile, the left-side tires usually support more weight, because that's the driver's side.

The problem is, if left in the same corner of the car, one tire will wear out much faster than the others just because of where it is. To prevent the tires from wearing unevenly, and to get longer life out of a set of tires, plan on having your tires rotated at least twice a year.

By rotating, we're talking about moving the tires from where they are to a different corner of the car. That allows them to wear more evenly, which should help them last longer. How you rotate them depends on what type of drivetrain your car has. In general, manufacturers recommend a modified X pattern. Here's what that means:

Rear-Wheel Drive — The rear tires move directly to the front, while the front tires should be switched side to side and then moved to the back.

Front-Wheel Drive — The front tires move directly to the back, while the rear tires should be switched side to side and then moved to the front.

Four-Wheel Drive or All-Wheel Drive — Both front and rear tires should be switched side to side and then moved to the opposite axle.

The only exception to these rotation directions is if your tires have a directional tread pattern. Most don't, but some — particularly those with special tread designed to channel water away quickly — are directional. If your tires have a directional tread, the tires must be moved front to back without switching sides.

Wheel Alignment and Balance

Traditional wisdom says that you should have your wheels aligned and tires balanced at least twice a year to get the most out of your tires. That's still true today. Aligning the wheels and balancing the tires regularly can increase your car's tire life considerably.

But here's a little food for thought: 25 years or so ago, a good set of radial tires cost $200-$300. An alignment and four-wheel balance cost $25 or $30 and, if performed regularly, could provide up to 40 percent more life out of the tires. So you'd pay about $180 over the life of the tires and pick up a considerable amount of additional tire life — a fair trade.

Today, a set of radial tires still costs between $200-$300 or maybe a few bucks more. Meanwhile, the price of an alignment and wheel balance has skyrocketed. You could easily pay $70 for an alignment and $30 or more for a four-wheel balance.

So an alignment and balance could cost $100 or more. If purchased six times over the life of the tires, that's more than $600 — twice the price of the tires. Meanwhile, the tires may still get up to 40 percent more life. All of a sudden, the tradeoff isn't all that great.

You still should have the wheels aligned and the tires balanced when you first have them put on the car. And if you experience a problem, such as unusual tire wear, vibration or steering problems, you should have the car checked and any necessary service performed.

Of course, it won't hurt anything to have the wheels aligned and the tires balanced more often than that. Maybe you'll want to have them done before going on vacation, just to avoid problems on the road. But from a purely financial sense, alignment and balance as maintenance may not be the smartest move you've ever made.

Checking Tire Condition

One of the easiest things you can do to protect yourself and your family is to check your tires now and then. Good tires provide the traction you need to drive and stop in all sorts of weather and road conditions. Worn or damaged tires can be a serious hazard.

The first step in checking your tires' condition is a visual inspection. Examine the tires, starting with the sidewalls. The sidewall should be relatively smooth and flat. Look for signs of bubbles, knots, gouges or cracks. If you aren't sure whether you're looking at a problem, assume it *is* a problem and have it examined professionally.

Then look at the tread, which should be even and fairly flat all the way across the tire. The front tires tend to wear slightly more on the edges than the back tires. That's normal, caused by the additional stress during turns. Here's what to look for when examining the tread:

1. **Single Edge Wear** – Indicates an alignment or suspension problem.
2. **Extreme Double Edge Wear** – Usually caused by low tire pressure.
3. **Center Tread Wear** – An uncommon problem, usually due to excessively high tire pressure.
4. **Feathered Wear** – When each tread is worn more on one edge than the other. An alignment problem caused by improper toe. The tires are scuffing down the road, causing the treads to wear this way.
5. **Cupping or Flat Spots** – Usually indicates a worn or loose component, or caused by a tire imbalance.
6. **Bubble or Tread Shifting to One Side** – Probably a belt or ply separation. This is a very dangerous condition, and you should have it checked immediately.
7. **Cuts, Gouges or Cracks** – Road hazard damage that should be checked for safety.
8. **Bald Band Evenly Across the Tread, Possibly Multiple Bands 8 to 12 Inches Apart** – This is normal wear. The bands are wear bars, designed to indicate when the tires are due for replacement. If you see the wear bars, take the car in and have the tires checked professionally.

WARNING
Be very careful handling or touching tires. Sharp objects can get caught in the tread, and exposed steel belts are extremely sharp. Either can cause a nasty, painful cut.

WARNING
A separated belt often will cause a severe wobble or vibration at very low speeds — usually under 15 mph. If you notice that type of wobble, have your tires checked immediately. Tires with shifted or separated belts can blow out unexpectedly and have been linked to a number of serious accidents and traffic fatalities.
Tip Provided by *Kevin Lane* *CAA Saskatchewan*

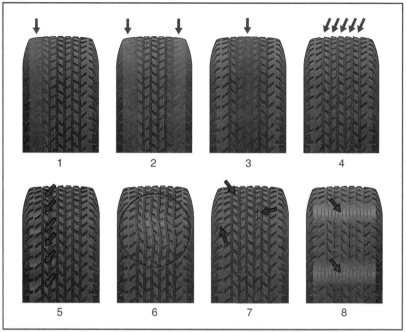

The specific pattern or condition indicates why the tire wore in a particular way and can help the technician find a problem in the steering or suspension.

IMPORTANT

Make sure you don't measure the tread depth against the wear bar.

Measuring Tread Depth

New passenger car tires will have 12/32 of an inch tread depth. This is the number the dealer or repair shop uses when calculating how much tread is worn away for inspection or warranty information.

The best way to measure the amount of tread left on the tire is to use a depth gauge made specifically for tires. This is just a small pin gauge, calibrated in thirty-seconds of an inch. You can get one at any auto parts store for just a couple of dollars. To measure the tread depth:

- Press the gauge all the way in to force the pin all the way out.
- Slip the pin into the tire tread and press down so the gauge bottoms.
- Lift the gauge away from the tire and read the depth on the gauge.
- Repeat the procedure in a second location at least 15 inches from the first measurement.

The tread depth is the average of the two readings. In general, $^{12}/_{32}$ of an inch is new; $^{7}/_{32}$ of an inch is half-worn; $^{2}/_{32}$ of an inch is worn out and should be replaced.

Measuring Tread Depth

The only really accurate way to check tread depth is with a depth gauge, available at any auto parts store.

Changing a Flat, Step by Step

You come out one morning and find one corner of the car sitting lower than the rest. You have a flat tire. If you want, go back inside, call for AAA emergency road service and have another cup of coffee while you wait. Don't want to wait, or no phone around? No problem. Changing a tire isn't all that difficult. Here's how:

Step

1 Check the spare tire. If it appears flat, see about getting it filled or fixed before you go any further.

2 Remove the spare tire, jack, T-wrench and wheel chocks from the trunk.

3 Slip the wheel chocks in place. Put them on both sides of the tire at the corner of the car opposite the flat. If you have four chocks, chock both wheels on the opposite axle.

TECH TIP

Chances are, you're familiar with the old "Lincoln cent" test. That's the one where you use a Lincoln one-cent piece to check the tread. (If you can see Lincoln's head, the tread is worn out.) This really isn't a good way to check tread depth. If your tires fail this test, they should have been replaced about six months ago.

Always obey these four basic safety rules when changing a tire:

1. Always try to have the car on a level surface. If necessary, drive the car a few feet on the flat tire to get it onto a level area.

2. If you're driving when the tire goes flat, make sure you get your car as far off the road as possible. Set up flares or reflective triangles about 75 to 100 feet behind the car to warn other motorists that you're there.

3. Never trust a jack. When a car is up on a jack, it's unsafe. Never climb under the car, or slide your arms or legs underneath while it's jacked up. Be prepared to move out of the way in case the car falls off the jack.

4. Always use wheel chocks behind the wheels on the axle opposite the flat while the car is jacked up. That will keep the wheels from turning and may keep the car from rolling off the jack.

TECH TIP
Make sure you know which way the lugs turn. Most turn counter-clockwise to loosen and clockwise to tighten, but some go the opposite way.

4 Remove the wheel cover from the wheel. If your wheel covers have locks, make sure you remove them before attempting to pry the wheel cover off.

5 Break the wheel lugs loose *before* you jack the car up. The time to fight with tight lugs is while the car is still firmly on the ground.

6 Jack the car up. If you're using the jack that came with the car, always follow the directions in your owner's manual or on the sticker in your trunk. Keep jacking the car up until the wheel is off the ground.

7 Use your T-wrench to remove the lug nuts one at a time. As you remove each one, lay it in the wheel cover to keep from losing it.

8 Once you have the lugs removed, remove the flat tire. You can use your T-wrench as a lever to help lift the tire off of the lugs and lower it to the ground.

The T-wrench can help you raise or lower a tire into position.

TECH TIP

Sometimes those wheel lugs get awfully tight. If you can't loosen them by hand, try lifting on one side of the T-wrench while pressing on the other end with your foot.

Tip Provided by
Dick Stigberg
AAA Northway

9 Mount the spare onto the wheel lugs. You can use your T-wrench as a lever to help lift the tire into place. You may have to jack the car up a little more to get the wheel on.

10 Start all of the wheel lug nuts by hand. Get them on a few threads before spinning them on with your T-wrench. Then spin them down evenly.

11 Once you have the lug nuts tightened down, lower the car onto the ground.

12 Use your T-wrench to tighten the lug nuts the rest of the way.

Don't worry about installing the hubcap or wheel cover: Just put it in the trunk for now. You're going to have to have your tire fixed and reinstalled, so have the shop reinstall the wheel cover while they reinstall the repaired tire.

13 Gather up all the tools and the flat tire, and put them in the trunk. If the chocks are stuck, you can loosen them by moving the car a little bit in the opposite direction.

That's all there is to changing a flat tire.

TECH TIP

Nothing is more useless than a flat spare tire or a spare you can't get to. To make sure your spare is ready when you need it, check the pressure regularly and make sure you can remove it from its mounting. Have any frozen or rusted mounting hardware cleaned, repaired or lubricated — before you have a flat tire.

Tip Provided by
Brad Ellsworth
AAA Southern New England

CHAPTER

12

Stopping on a Dime: All About the Brakes

In This Chapter

- An introduction to brake systems and their components

- How antilock-brake systems work and how to get the most out of them

- Choosing the right brake fluid

- Maintaining your car's brake system

- What to do if the brakes fail

You're driving down the road, and the traffic light turns red. You let up on the gas, gently apply the brakes, and the car slowly comes to a stop. It's not much wonder that most folks think that brakes stop the car.

But actually, the brakes only stop the wheels. Think that's just a matter of semantics? Ask anyone who's ever slammed on the brakes, only to end up sliding through the light and right into oncoming traffic.

Braking is a carefully constructed balance between the brakes and the contact between the tires and the roadway. If one brake applies more stopping force than the others, the consequences could be catastrophic.

This also is why most manufacturers now offer antilock brakes on their cars. These brake systems actually measure the speed of the wheels and adapt system pressure to prevent any one wheel from breaking loose from the roadway. The result is a braking system that won't lock the wheels so you can maintain control of your car even during the most critical braking situations.

In this chapter, you'll learn about the brake system on your car. And you'll learn about the service necessary to keep your car's brakes working properly, so that when you need them, they'll be ready.

Brake System Overview

Brakes work by taking advantage of the properties of friction to slow the wheels. A smooth metal object mounts to the wheels and rotates with them; a softer object mounts to the car's suspension. When you apply the brakes, the soft object presses against the harder one, dragging against it to slow the wheels.

Brakes come in two common forms: drum and disk. Drum brakes consist of a set of brake shoes, which mount to the car's suspension. These brake shoes are curved metal plates, with a soft friction material bonded or riveted to them. A metal drum slides over the shoes and mounts to the wheel. As you press on the brake pedal, the brake shoes move out to contact the brake drum. They rub against the drum, creating friction and slowing the wheel.

Drum Brake Assembly

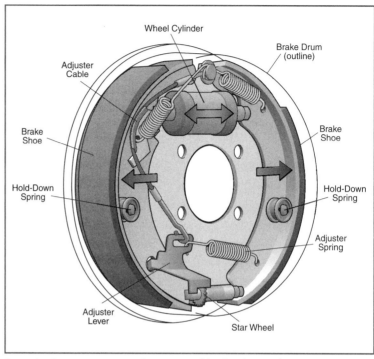

Wheel Cylinder

Brake Drum
(outline)

Adjuster
Cable

Brake
Shoe

Brake
Shoe

Hold-Down
Spring

Hold-Down
Spring

Adjuster
Spring

Adjuster
Lever

Star Wheel

Drum brakes press out against a round brake drum when you press on the brake pedal, creating friction and slowing the wheels.

Disk brakes work a little differently. Disk brakes consist of two flat pads that mount inside a large caliper. These are the disk brake pads, which are flat metal plates with a soft friction material riveted to them. The caliper bolts to the car's suspension. A flat disk, or rotor, bolts to the wheel. When you press the brake pedal, the caliper presses against the brake pads, which squeeze the rotor between them. This creates the friction to slow the wheel.

When repair technicians tell you your car's brakes need replacing, it's these brake shoes or pads they're talking about. The brake shoes and pads are designed to wear out. That's why they're softer than the drums or rotors. They wear out so the drums and rotors won't.

Disk Brake Assembly

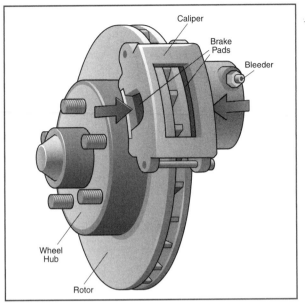

Disk brakes squeeze the brake rotor between two pads to create the friction to stop the wheels.

In recent years, manufacturers have had to change the material used for the brake shoes and pads. Instead of using asbestos, they've switched to a composite of metal shavings mixed into a resin. This material still provides the friction surface necessary to stop the car. In fact, it's even better than the old asbestos pads, because it handles heat better to prevent the brakes from fading when they heat up.

But today, more than ever before, that brake friction material does cause the brake drums and rotors to wear. That's why your repair shop also may recommend resurfacing the drums and rotors: to even out the wear on their surfaces and provide a flat surface for the brakes to press against.

Brake Hydraulic Systems

To transfer the pressure your foot applies to the brake pedal, auto manufacturers use a hydraulic system. This system takes advantage of the properties of a fluid – called *brake fluid* – to transfer the pedal movement to the wheels and apply the brakes.

Here's how it works: When you press the brake pedal, you're actually moving a piston inside a device called a *master cylinder*. The master cylinder is filled with brake fluid. As you press on the brakes, the piston in the master cylinder moves, which forces the brake fluid through a series of steel lines and reinforced rubber hoses.

TECH TIP Many disk brake pads come with "squealers" — wear indicators designed to create a noise similar to nails on a blackboard. If you start to hear a high-pitched squealing noise coming from the wheels, take your car in and have the brakes checked. Don't wait: A few thousand miles, and that squeal will turn into a grind and end up costing a lot more to fix.

Tip Provided by
David Allen
Automobile Club of
Southern California

Master Cylinder

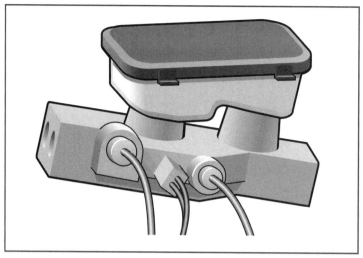

An important property of fluids in liquid form is they won't com-press. So when you press on the brakes and move the piston in the master cylinder, the fluid transfers that movement directly to the brakes. That movement causes a second series of pistons at the wheels to move. On drum brakes, these pistons sit inside a wheel cylinder. On disk brakes, it's in the caliper. In each case, the movement causes the piston to move, which applies the brakes.

Brake Hydraulic System

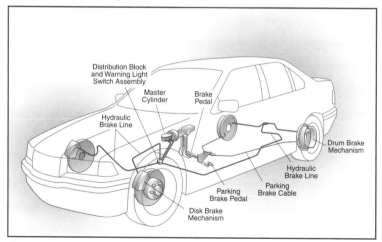

The master cylinder supplies the pressure to the system that actuates the disk and drum brakes.

Brake hydraulic systems also include other valves, such as metering valves, proportioning valves and combination valves. These valves help balance the pressure within the brake system to make sure the brakes apply in the correct time and proportion between the front and rear.

Most cars today also include a power brake booster. This is a vacuum or hydraulically controlled device that mounts between the master cylinder and the firewall to increase the force your foot applies to the brakes. This simply makes it easier to apply the brakes, so you don't have to press the pedal as hard.

Emergency Brakes

In addition to the regular service brakes, your car has an emergency brake. This is either a pedal or lever, designed to allow you to apply part of the brake system if the regular brakes fail. The lever or pedal connects to a cable, which in turn connects to part of the regular brake system, usually on the rear brakes. When you press the pedal or pull up on the lever, the cable pulls against a separate actuator to apply the brakes.

While the emergency brake is far less efficient than the regular brakes, it will stop the car in the event the regular brakes fail. And it's useful for helping keep the car from rolling when you park. But there is a downside to the emergency brakes. Since they only actuate half the brakes, using the emergency brake to stop the car is much more likely to cause the wheels to lock. If you have to use the emergency brake to stop the car, always apply it gently and be prepared to release it slightly.

Antilock Brake Systems

The biggest change to come along to the brake systems in years is the introduction of antilock brakes. This is a computerized system that monitors wheel speed during braking. If one wheel slows too quickly, the system activates a series of valves and pumps to adjust the brake pressure hundreds of times a second. This lowers the brake pressure so the wheel can begin turning again.

You can feel it and hear it, too. If you slam down on the brake pedal while the car's moving, you can feel the vibration, both in the brake pedal and the car itself. It's like the brakes are applying and releasing, over and over again. And that's just what's happening.

CAUTION

Be careful using the emergency brake in cold weather when parked. Emergency brakes have been known to freeze while on, preventing the car from moving. If that happens, you'll probably have to have the car towed into a shop to be thawed out.

Typical ABS System

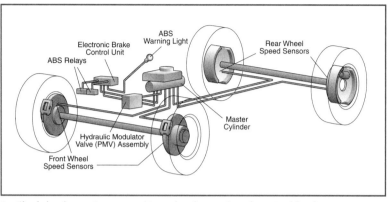

Antilock-brake systems monitor wheel speed and control brake pressure to prevent the brakes from locking up. This provides you with full steering control, even when the brakes are applied full force.

Many people believe that antilock brake systems allow the car to stop faster than normal brakes. This is true in some instances but not in others. Actually, the reason for antilock brakes has little to do with how quickly the car comes to a stop.

Here's the problem: When your car's brakes lock up, you lose something more than just braking control. You also lose steering control. Ask anyone who's ever been in an accident. Once the wheels lock, it no longer matters which way you turn the wheel. The car is going to keep moving in the direction of momentum; that is, the direction it was traveling. Turning the steering wheel won't change anything.

This is where antilock brake systems really make a difference. Since the antilock brake system won't let the wheels lock, you maintain control of the steering. This enables you to avoid accidents while still holding the brakes to the floor.

Antilock brake systems were designed to reduce accidents, but in many cases just the opposite has happened. More accidents occurred, not because of a brake problem, but because car owners were frightened by the vibration when they slammed on the brake pedal. So they backed off on the brakes and ran into other cars.

The best way to avoid that situation is to become familiar with the ABS system. Find an open, deserted road and go for a drive. Then slam on the brakes. Get acquainted with how they feel when they're controlling the brake pressure. That way, when you need to stop in a hurry, you won't be afraid of how the brakes feel.

The Most Ignored Fluid

Everyone knows about engine oil, transmission fluid, engine coolant and even windshield washer solvent. But one fluid that gets ignored or forgotten more than any other is the brake fluid. That's strange, because low brake fluid can cause you to lose braking altogether — not a particularly good situation.

Brake fluid is a very special fluid, with a number of specific requirements:

1. It must work with a wide range of materials, without affecting them. These materials include steel, iron, aluminum, copper, brass and special rubber compounds, all found within the brake hydraulic system.

2. It must withstand extreme temperatures and rapid pressure changes without freezing or boiling.

3. It must absorb moisture to protect the system and prevent the moisture from freezing or boiling.

4. It must provide lubrication for the moving parts within the braking system.

That's a pretty tall order for any single fluid, but brake fluids meet those challenges to keep your car's brake system working properly in all kinds of conditions. Brake fluids come in several different ratings, based predominately on their resistance to boiling. You can identify these fluids by their Department of Transportation rating:

Fluid Rating	Dry Boiling Point	Wet Boiling Point*
DOT 3	401° F (205° C)	284° F (140° C)
DOT 4	446° F (230° C)	311° F (155° C)
DOT 5	500° F (260° C)	356° F (180° C)
DOT 5.1	518° F (270° C)	375° F (190° C)

* Brake fluid containing 3 percent moisture

DOT 3, 4 and 5.1 are *poly glycol ether*-based fluids. DOT 5 is a silicone-based fluid. Most car brake systems require DOT 3 brake fluid. Brake fluids with a DOT 4 or DOT 5.1 rating usually will also meet DOT 3 ratings and will say so right on the bottle.

How can you be sure what type of brake fluid your car takes? Check the reservoir. It should have the brake fluid requirement molded or stamped right into the reservoir or cap. Most use DOT 3.

Changing the Brake Fluid

The biggest problem brake fluids have to deal with is moisture. Brake fluids are *hydroscopic* — that is, they attract and absorb moisture. If they didn't, you could end up with small pockets of water in the brake system. Those pockets could freeze in cold weather or could boil and turn to steam when the system was operating normally. Either condition could compromise the brake system's operation.

But as the brake fluid absorbs moisture, its boiling temperature drops. Just 3 percent moisture in the brake fluid will lower its boiling point by over a third. What's more, that moisture can separate from the brake fluid, condensing on brake components. That condensation can rust the metals inside the brake system, and in cold weather, that condensation can freeze on rubber brake parts. That's why repair shops get a rush on brake failures the first cold day of each year.

If that weren't bad enough, today's antilock brake systems are even more susceptible to moisture damage. The switches, valves and solenoids in those brake systems have much tighter tolerances than standard brake systems, so even a light coating of rust or dirt will affect their operation.

To prevent those problems and to keep your car's brake system in top condition, you should have your car's brake fluid changed at least every couple of years.

Changing the brake fluid isn't a job you can do at home. In most cars, it requires special brake bleeding tools and equipment to force out the old fluid and bleed out any air left in the system. A regular brake fluid change will help keep your car's brakes in good working order for years to come.

Brake System Maintenance

There are three types of maintenance that should be performed on your car's brake system:

- Check the brake fluid level.
- Inspect the brake system.
- Replace the brake fluid.

Only one of these procedures — checking the brake fluid level — is a procedure you can perform yourself. The other two should be left to a qualified repair technician. Inspecting the brakes usually involves removing the wheels and examining the brakes, hydraulic system and hardware for signs of wear or damage. In most cases, you should have the brakes checked every six months. Many states require a safety inspection, which usually includes a visual examination of the brake system.

Another check that some states now include in their inspection procedure is a dynamic brake test. This involves driving over a set of sensors and hitting the brakes. The tester then displays what percentage of braking each wheel is providing. Dynamic brake testing is a great way to make sure your car's brakes are balanced and working properly.

Many people believe that changing the brake fluid is some type of scam, designed to separate you from your paycheck. But as we discussed earlier, brake fluids absorb moisture, which can damage the brake system and reduce braking effectiveness. The only way to remove that moisture is to have the brake fluid changed. In most cases, you should have your car's brake fluid changed every two years or so.

TECH TIP

Brake fluids don't just absorb moisture while in the brake system. They also can absorb moisture while still in the bottle. To prevent contaminating the brake fluid while it's still on the shelf, always close the bottle after use and keep it capped tightly while storing it.

Checking the Brake Fluid

Most repair shops check the brake fluid during an oil change, but it's a good idea to check it yourself at the same time you check the oil level. To check your car's brake fluid level:

CAUTION

Never allow brake fluid to drip on your car's finish. The brake fluid will soften and remove the paint. If you accidentally drip brake fluid on the finish, flush it with plain water immediately.

1. Locate the master cylinder. It's usually under the hood, right in line with the steering wheel. If you can't find the master cylinder, check your owner's manual.

2. Use a clean rag to wipe off the top of the master cylinder. Make sure it's clean and dry before opening the reservoir.

3. Check what type of fluid the system uses. The fluid type will be stamped or molded into the reservoir or the fill cap.

4. Open the reservoir. How you do this depends on what type of master cylinder reservoir you have. Some will have a screw cap; on others, the cap will snap down into place. Older cars may use a spring clip that snaps over the cap. To remove that type, you'll need a screwdriver to snap the spring clip off of the cap.

5. Check the fluid level. If it's low, add a little fluid to bring the level up to the full mark. If there's no full mark, add fluid until it's about one-quarter of an inch from the top of the reservoir.

Different Types of Master Cylinder Cap

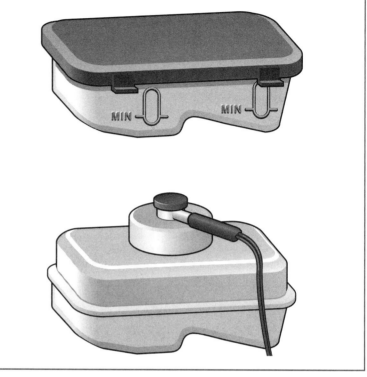

There are many master cylinders on the market, each with its own type of cap. If you aren't sure how to open the master cylinder on your car, check the owner's manual or ask your local technician.

6   Reset the rubber seal in the cap. This seal is designed to pop out and fill the empty space in the master cylinder. Tuck it back into place before reinstalling the cap.

7   Reinstall the cap. Make sure it's seated properly and locked into place.

If Your Brake Light Comes On

First things first: Never drive the car unless you're sure the brakes are working OK. If you even think there *may* be a problem, pull over and call for emergency roadside assistance.

To isolate the problem, start by checking your emergency brake. Apply and release it a couple of times and see if the light goes out. If your car has an emergency brake pedal, try lifting up on the pedal while you pull on the release. If the light remains on, open the hood and check your brake fluid. If it's low, try adding to it. Refer to the section on brakes for more details about brake fluid and how to add it. If both the emergency brake and brake fluid seem fine, assume the problem is a hydraulic system failure. Don't try to drive the car until that's fixed.

If Your Brakes Stop Working

Hopefully you read through this section before your brakes stopped working. The time to read this *isn't* while speeding along the highway with your brake pedal on the floor. But if your brakes stop working, there are a number of things you can do to slow and even stop your car:

1 **Pump the Brake Pedal** — Brake failures can be caused by air in the lines or a master cylinder problem. Pumping the brake pedal sometimes can build up enough pressure in the system to get the brakes working momentarily.

2 **Shift into Low Gear** — On an automatic transmission, put the shifter into manual low (usually all the way at the end of the shift indicator). The transmission will make a mechanical connection, and the engine will slow the car. On a manual transmission, dropping into first gear does the same thing.

3 **Apply the Emergency Brake** — The emergency brake uses a cable to apply one-half of the brakes (usually the rears). While not nearly as effective as the regular service brakes, the emergency brake can stop the car.

Once you have your car stopped, don't try to drive any farther. Roll the car off the road and park it. Then call for a tow truck to come and get it.

CAUTION

Don't put the transmission in park. That'll just make a lot of noise and probably damage the transmission.

CHAPTER

13

Air Conditioning and Heating: Driving in Comfort

In This Chapter

• • • • • • • • • • • •

- An introduction to typical air conditioning and heating systems

- Different types of refrigerants and why they're necessary

- Adjusting the A/C system for optimum performance

- Maintaining your car's A/C system

At the end of the 19th century, when men like Duryea, Buick and Daimler began designing the first cars, they had one thing in mind: to build a mechanical device that would get you from here to there. Not much thought was given to your comfort during the ride. If you wanted to stay warm in cold weather, you wore a heavier coat.

Then one day, someone had an idea: If they piped some of the hot water from the engine into a small heat exchanger — like the radiator, only smaller — and mounted that heat exchanger in the passenger compartment, the passengers could receive heat in the wintertime.

There have been a few improvements since those first heaters appeared, but the heaters in today's cars work virtually the same as those first ones did almost a hundred years ago. Almost 50 years would pass before someone figured out how to take advantage of the laws of physics to transfer heat from the passenger compartment to the outside air and call it "air conditioning."

Today's cars offer advanced climate control systems designed to anticipate temperature demand and adjust their operation to provide a comfortable environment under just about any conditions. There are even some systems that provide zone controls to allow the passenger to enjoy one temperature setting while the driver can choose a different one.

In this chapter, we'll look at today's air conditioning and heating systems — how they work, the maintenance they require and how to adjust them to provide the most efficient operation.

System Overview

The heaters in today's cars aren't all that different from those first heaters that appeared so many years ago. They still use engine coolant to warm the passenger compartment through a small heat exchanger, called a *heater core*.

While the heater captures heat from the engine, there's no place for the air conditioning to capture "cool." So to cool the air, air conditioning systems use refrigerant. Refrigerants have a special property that makes them useful in an air conditioning system. They're condensable; that is, they can be forced to change states from a liquid to a vapor and back again, at common temperatures. This property allows refrigerants to transfer far more heat than they could simply through expansion and compression. Let's look at a typical system and see how this works.

The A/C system is divided into two halves: a high side and a low side. A large pump, called a *compressor*, starts the refrigerant moving, while an *expansion valve* creates a restriction, allowing pressure to build on one side – the high side – while causing it to drop on the low side. It's this change in pressure that causes the refrigerant to absorb and release heat.

As the high-pressure liquid refrigerant passes through the expansion valve, the sudden drop in pressure forces the refrigerant to expand. This expansion requires the refrigerant to take on heat. The only way it can do that is to become colder than the air around it.

Air Conditioning System

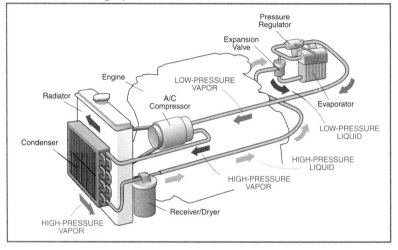

The cold refrigerant enters a heat exchanger called an *evaporator*. Here the cold refrigerant takes on heat from the air, which allows it to boil and change from a liquid to a vapor. This is how the A/C system takes heat out of the air entering the passenger compartment.

From there, the refrigerant goes to the compressor, which pumps it through, raising its pressure. To condense back into a liquid, the refrigerant now must release heat: This time it can only do so by becoming hot. The hot refrigerant enters another heat exchanger that sits in front of the car called a *condenser*. Outside air passes over the condenser fins, removing the heat, and allowing the refrigerant to condense back to a liquid. From here it continues back to the expansion valve to begin the process all over again.

There are some other considerations and components, such as a process for maintaining system pressures and a dryer for capturing water from the refrigerant. But in general terms, this is how all A/C and refrigeration systems work.

Refrigerants, Then and Now

For years, when anyone talked about charging their air conditioning system, they were talking about R12, sometimes called *Freon*® — DuPont's trade name for R12.

What made R12 such a good refrigerant is that it's a condensable chemical; that is, it can be forced to change from a liquid to a gas and back to a liquid at normal temperatures. That's the key to absorbing and transferring large amounts of heat from one area to another.

But back in the 1960s, scientists began to suspect a problem with R12. They noticed that ultraviolet radiation from the sun had been increasing due to a reduction in ozone in the upper atmosphere. Testing indicated that this was due to a class of chemicals called *chlorofluorocarbons*, or CFC's. R12 is a CFC.

Further testing and examination of the ozone layer indicated the Earth was at serious risk from ultraviolet radiation, which has been linked to skin cancers, reduced crop yields and other life-threatening consequences. To protect the planet, the United States joined with other industrial nations to sign the Montreal Protocol, which banned the use of CFC's and set dates to end its manufacture. In addition, repair centers now are required to recover and recycle R12 instead of releasing it into the atmosphere.

Most cars built since 1996 have been using a new refrigerant: R134a. R134a also is a condensable chemical, but tests show it to be safe for the ozone layer. And by following the necessary procedures, technicians can adapt older R12 systems to use R134a.

R134a has two problems when being used to replace R12. Its smaller molecular structure allows it to leak more easily than R12. So if your car's A/C system has a tiny leak with R12, R134a will leak much faster. And in some cases, R134a can seep out of hoses that were able to contain R12 fairly well. At high temperatures, its pressure is considerably higher than R12. So in extremely high temperatures, the system may reach pressures too high to operate efficiently. But careful tests, repairs and retrofit procedures can negate these problems.

Today, there are three types of refrigerant on the market: R12, R134a and blends. Which should you use in your car? It depends on what's in there now. If your car uses R134a, the choice is simple: Stick with it. The refrigerant in your car's A/C system is the latest available, the system is designed to use it efficiently, and the price for it is dropping all the time.

If your car uses R12, you have a couple of choices. You can continue to use R12. There's still a lot of old stock out there, as well as the recycled R12 that's available. And nothing works better in a system designed for R12 than R12.

The down side is cost: The price of R12 is rising all the time. Some people have paid as much as $80 a pound for it, so a simple A/C system charge can cost hundreds of dollars. If you're planning to keep your car for several more years, you may want to think about having it retrofitted for R134a. If performed properly, a retrofitted system should provide adequate cooling under most conditions.

What about the blends? These are mixtures of R12, R22 (the refrigerant used in your home air conditioner or refrigerator) and other chemicals. Your best bet: Steer clear of them. There are two reasons to avoid blends:

First, since there are no real standards for their composition, there's no way for anyone to work on your car's A/C system without draining what's in it and starting over. Otherwise, they couldn't be sure whether the system operating pressures are high or low. Second and most important, some blends contain chemicals such as propane and butane — both highly flammable and dangerous in an accident. So, in general, you have two choices with an older A/C system: Stick with R12 or retrofit for R134a. Forget about the blends.

Charging Practices: It Isn't Like the Old Days

If you've been driving for more than a few years, you may remember when it was a normal practice to take your car in every spring to have the air conditioning charged. A little squirt of R12 until the sight glass was clear, and you were good for another year.

Back then, R12 was cheap: $2 or $3 a pound, and $12 would fill nearly any system out there. Even if you had a little leak, so what? A pound or two, and you were as good as new. A lot of things have changed since then. To begin with, today's A/C systems don't leak unless they have a real problem.

And the sight glass? Only a few cars have them, and they're only there to allow the technician to see whether the refrigerant is actually flowing. They're *supposed* to have bubbles in them. In fact, if you filled one of today's A/C systems until the bubbles were gone, it'd be so overfull that it wouldn't cool and might even damage the compressor.

In addition, refrigerant prices have gone through the roof. Some shops are charging $80 or more for a pound of R12. So the fill-and-go doesn't make nearly as much sense as it did a few years ago.

Adding refrigerant to a leaking system isn't good for the environment. Some studies indicate that R12 may be a contributing factor to the deterioration of the Earth's ozone layer. And while research indicates that R134a does not directly impact the ozone, this refrigerant is identified as a greenhouse gas.

That's why any reputable repair shop will refuse to fill a leaking A/C system. Instead, they'll insist on performing a leak check and repairing the system properly. And instead of venting the old refrigerant into the atmosphere, they now use recovery and recycling equipment to capture, clean and reuse refrigerants.

So if your air conditioning isn't working up to par, don't expect a quick, cheap fill-up-and-go: Today's A/C technicians will check the system for leaks, recover and recycle the old refrigerant, repair the system, and recharge it to factory specs. And that should bring your car's A/C system up to like-new operating performance.

Adjusting the System for Optimum Performance

You might think that setting the air conditioning or heating system would be a pretty simple procedure, but you'd be amazed at how many cars get taken in for repairs, just because the car owners didn't have the A/C system set properly. Obviously, one of the first places to look for this information is in your owner's manual. But there are a few tips you should be aware of that will help you get the most out of your car's A/C system.

First, remember that warm air rises and cold air sinks. That means in most cases you'll want to use the floor vents for the heat. In the warm weather you should use the panel vents for the A/C, and you should adjust them to aim slightly upward. That way the air will circulate better and cool the passenger compartment more quickly.

Once the temperature in the passenger compartment becomes comfortable, don't just shut the system off because you'll only have to turn it back on in a few minutes. Instead, adjust the temperature slightly and lower the fan speed. That'll keep it comfortable inside.

To defrost or defog your windows in the winter, the defroster is a good choice. But windows can become fogged on damp summer days, too. On those days, switch to the A/C, set to normal. The A/C system dries the air coming in and will circulate it better than the defroster.

Don't switch to the maximum setting on the A/C to defog your windows. That setting recirculates the air in the passenger compartment so cool, dry air may not reach all the way to the windows. The normal setting works better. On really hot days, you may want to use the max A/C setting. On most cars max A/C shuts off any coolant flow through the heater core and recycles the air in the passenger compartment instead of trying to cool and dehumidify the outside air. But don't leave it on max too long. Eventually the air inside will become stuffy and can affect your concentration. Once the system has taken the edge off the heat, switch to normal.

Air Conditioning System Maintenance

Your car's air conditioning is the one system that probably doesn't require a lot of regular maintenance. In general, if the system's working, it's OK. If not, it needs to be checked and repaired.

There are a few simple checks you can perform to keep the A/C working properly or determine whether it needs to be serviced:

Check the Condenser — That's the large heat exchanger in the front of your car, just forward of the radiator. Take a look at it and make sure there's no dirt or debris blocking air flow through it. Remove any litter that's attached itself to the condenser and use a garden hose to wash away any dirt or bugs that are stuck on.

Check the Belt — With the engine off, check the compressor belt for wear and make sure it's tight. If it's too loose or damaged, have it tightened or replaced before the summer gets into full swing.

Watch out for sharp edges around the condenser. You could cut yourself on the condenser fins or the metal brackets around it.

*Tip Provided by
Robert C. Knop
Ohio Motorists Association*

Checking the Condenser

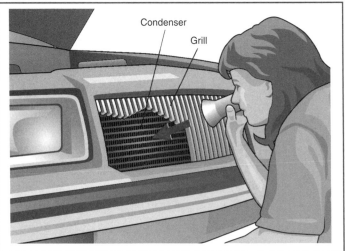

Condenser

Grill

Checking the A/C Belt

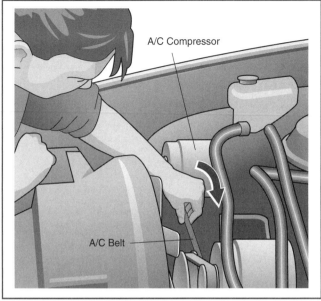

Check the Operation – Start the engine and try the A/C on the first warm day.

- Do you hear any strange noises?
- If your car has an electric cooling fan, does it start when you turn on the A/C? (It should on most cars.)
- Is cold air coming out of the vents?
- Try the controls: Does the air come out of the correct vents?

If everything seems OK, your air conditioning probably will work fine for the season. But if you notice a problem during any of these checks, take your car in to have the system checked and repaired.

Check the Air Filter – Some of today's cars have an air filter to filter the air coming into the passenger compartment. It may be called a *pollen filter*, a *particulate filter* or a *micron filter*. Whatever it's called, if your car has one, you should check it and replace it if it's dirty. If you're not sure if your car has an A/C system air filter, check your owner's manual. It'll tell you whether it has one, where to find it and how to check it.

CHAPTER

14

Emission Controls and Testing: Protecting the Planet

In This Chapter
• • • • • • • • • • • •

- An introduction to typical emission control systems

- An introduction to emission testing

- How to prepare for an emissions test

- What to do if your car fails emissions

- Waivers and warranties: How do they apply to you?

Today's cars are cleaner and more efficient than at any other time in history. Automakers still are being pressured to further reduce the emissions from their vehicles. That's why manufacturers are looking to special low-emission vehicles, electric cars and hybrids to help reduce vehicle emissions.

In this chapter, we'll look at some of the ways auto manufacturers address auto emissions. And we'll discuss some of the tests now in use to identify polluting vehicles.

Emission Devices Do More than Just Clean the Air

Over the years, auto manufacturers have used all kinds of devices to help reduce emissions. The most common of these devices reads like an explosion at the alphabet soup kitchen: PCV, EGR, EVAP, AIR, and the list goes on and on.

Many people would have you believe that these emissions devices were costing you money and that disconnecting them would increase gas mileage. Nothing could be further from the truth.

Let's take a look at some of the more common devices. We'll learn what the abbreviations stand for and what they do to help reduce emissions.

A Typical PCV System

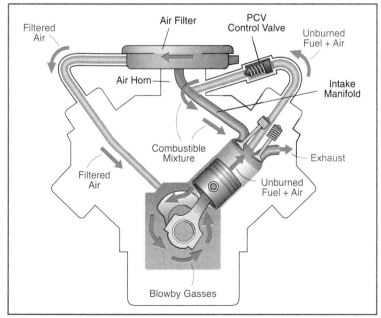

The PCV system pulls unburned fuel vapors out of the crankcase and back into the intake, where the engine gets a second chance at burning them.

PCV – Positive crankcase ventilation valve. The PCV valve draws unburned gasoline vapors that get past the pistons back into the intake to give the engine a second chance to burn them. This helps prevent unburned hydrocarbons from escaping into the atmosphere.

EGR – Exhaust gas recirculation valve. A vacuum or electric valve that redirects a small amount of exhaust gas back into the engine's intake. The object is to reduce the amount of volatile gasses in the combustion chamber to lower combustion temperatures. This prevents ping or knock and helps reduce NOx levels.

EVAP – Evaporative emission system. A surprising amount of emissions from cars is caused strictly by evaporation. Raw gas vaporizes and escapes as hydrocarbon emissions. To prevent this, the EVAP system redirects fuel vapors into a charcoal canister to store them. Then, when the engine is warmed up and running, the system releases these stored vapors into the intake to be burned during normal combustion.

AIR – Air injection reaction. This is the air pump that many cars use to pump fresh air into the exhaust system. This fresh air enables unburned or incompletely burned exhaust to continue burning, before it escapes the exhaust system. While some cars use a belt-driven pump, many others use a special pump that uses the exhaust's natural flow to pull air in. And some cars now are using electric pumps for the same purpose.

CAT – Catalytic converter. The catalytic converter is a type of chemical afterburner. By reacting to the exhaust gasses, it helps reduce emission levels by giving them one last chance to burn before they leave the tailpipe. On newer cars, catalytic converters also help reduce NOx by separating the nitrogen and oxygen in a process called "reduction."

As you can see, most of these devices actually serve to improve gas mileage. Even the catalytic converter tends to be passive when discussing fuel economy. Only the AIR system – and only on some cars – puts any load on the engine, and it's a minimal one at that. So if someone tells you that they can improve your car's gas mileage by disconnecting the emission controls, smile knowingly and say thanks, but no thanks.

Emission Testing Programs

Nearly 40 states now have some form of enhanced emissions program in place. These tests usually involve several inspection procedures:

- Emission device tampering
- Dynamometer testing to examine the exhaust emission levels under simulated road conditions

- Gas cap test
- Evaporative system pressure and purge test (some states only)
- Onboard diagnostic self-test (some states only)

The limits for these tests usually are considerably more lenient than the car was designed to pass. The object is to identify "gross polluters" and to require them to be repaired.

Does Your Car Require Emissions Inspection?

In general, you'll receive some type of notification from the state indicating whether your car has to be tested. It either will come as a requirement for renewing your car's registration or as a notice with your registration, indicating the requirement. In that case, the inspection station usually will put a sticker on your windshield indicating that the car passed the emissions test.

But just because the state sends you a notice doesn't automatically mean you're required to have an emissions inspection. Most states offer waivers for certain conditions:

- Low Annual Mileage – If you drive your car less than 5,000 miles a year, you may be eligible for a low mileage waiver.
- Senior Citizens – Some states offer senior citizen waivers for emissions inspection.

There may be others, so check with your state's department of transportation or go to their website and look for information on their auto emissions testing program.

Preparing for Emissions Inspection

Assuming your car does have to have an emissions inspection, what should you do to prepare for it? There are a few things you can do ahead of time to help speed things along:

Check Tire Condition and Pressure — The inspection station may refuse to test a car with tires it deems unsafe. Low or uneven tire pressure could affect your car's emission results by affecting the speed rating on the dynamometer.

Make Sure Gas Cap is Tight — Depending on your state's program, a loose cap could cause your car to fail the evaporative test. Even if it isn't part of the test, checking the gas cap isn't a bad idea.

Check for Severe Leaks — The inspection station may refuse to inspect a car with a severe, obvious leak — the type that drips on the floor while you're standing there. If you notice a leak of this type, have it fixed before you bother taking the car in for inspection.

One thing you shouldn't do in most cases is have your car tuned or the fuel system serviced before the initial inspection. This seems counterintuitive, but there's a reason: Every state is required to provide a repair limit waiver to limit the amount you have to spend to repair the car. The problem is, some states don't count work done immediately before the inspection. Get these services done after the inspection to restore driveability and fuel economy and to minimize exhaust emissions.

However, one maintenance item you *should* have done before the emissions inspection is an oil change. That's because old engine oil can be contaminated with fuel vapors, which will increase emission levels. But an oil change usually won't count toward an emission waiver, so doing it ahead of time is a good idea.

Emissions Failures

Obviously, if your car passes the emissions test, you're all done. The car gets its sticker or the registration gets renewed, and that's all there is to it until next year. But if your car fails inspection, then what? That depends on the nature of the failure.

- If your car fails for tampering, all bets are off. You have to have the car repaired, regardless of cost. Tampering isn't covered by waivers.
- If your car fails for a diluted exhaust sample, it indicates an exhaust leak or a problem with the AIR system. Either problem will have to be fixed before the car can be tested. Whether a waiver would cover either problem depends on the specific situation and the individual state.
- If your car fails for a leaking gas cap, you'll have to replace it. You can get a new one at any auto parts store, and replacing the cap is no more difficult than pumping your own gas.
- If your car fails due to excessive exhaust emissions, the repair you need depends on the specific exhaust failure. There are a lot of different possibilities for each type of failure, but, in general, these are the likely ones:

Carbon Monoxide (CO) — Indicates a rich mixture. For some reason the engine is getting more fuel than it can burn completely. The specific cause may depend on whether your car uses a carburetor or fuel injection.

Hydrocarbons (HC) — Indicates some type of misfire. Hydrocarbons are raw, unburned gas. High levels of hydrocarbon usually are due to an ignition problem or an internal engine problem, but extremely lean mixtures (low CO) also can cause high hydrocarbon levels.

Oxides of Nitrogen (NOx) — Indicates excessively high combustion temperatures. This often is caused by an inoperative EGR valve but can be caused by a few other possibilities as well, including carbon buildup in the combustion chamber.

Having Your Car Repaired

Where you take your car for emissions repairs is wide open. Many states certify certain shops to perform these repairs, but you aren't limited to take your car to one of these shops. You can take it anywhere, or you can even perform the repairs yourself.

The difference is what counts toward a waiver. That's because each state was required to limit the amount you spend on emissions repairs by offering a waiver. If your repairs go over a preset limit without repairing the failure — usually between $150 and $300 — they may have to pass your car with a waiver.

But there are a number of limitations to these waivers. For one thing, the repairs performed must be consistent with the failure. For example, a set of new tires wouldn't count toward an HC failure. On the other hand, a set of spark plugs probably would.

Another consideration is the labor cost. This is where taking your car to a certified emissions repair center comes in. If the repairs are performed by a certified center, the labor cost counts toward a waiver. If the repair shop isn't certified or you do them yourself, only the parts cost counts toward the waiver.

Emissions Warranties

Then again, do you even have to pay for the repairs? Not if your car is still covered by an emissions warranty. Federal law requires that manufacturers cover your car for emission failures far longer than many regular warranties.

Federal law states that all emission failures must be covered for the first two years or 24,000 miles. After that, cars built before 1995 are covered for specific emission components for five years or 50,000 miles; 1995-and-later cars are covered for eight years or 80,000 miles.

These warranties are only on specific components and are only valid if the components failed under normal use. Misuse or tampering failures will void the warranty. But if your car fails emissions, check your owner's manual. You may find the emissions warranty is still valid long after the regular repair warranty has expired.

TECH TIP

If you've had your car repaired and NOx levels still are high, you can cheat a little by switching to a slightly higher octane gas. Higher octane gas burns more slowly, so it tends to lower NOx levels. However, it also may increase your HC levels, so it isn't necessarily a good repair unless everything else is working perfectly.

Emissions Additives

When the enhanced emissions program was introduced, dozens of additives and chemicals began appearing in stores all across the country. These additives promised to make your car pass the emissions inspection, simply by adding a bottle to the gas tank or crankcase (depending on the additive). In some cases, these additives may help improve certain emission levels slightly by increasing the effective octane of the gas, or reducing engine blowby. In general, however, these offer a lot of empty promises.

One thing that will help reduce emissions on many cars is a good fuel and induction system service. This service helps lower carbon monoxide and hydrocarbons by cleaning the injectors to eliminate drips and improve the spray pattern. And they lower NOx levels by removing carbon from the combustion chamber. In some cases, this service actually can help rejuvenate the catalytic converter, reducing emissions even further.

But as we discussed in Chapter 6, a proper fuel system and induction service is only possible through a repair shop. The do-it-yourselfer kits available through most parts stores just aren't able to provide the level of cleaning necessary to make a real difference to your car's emission levels. To have your car's emission failure repaired, you will want to take it to a qualified repair center.

CHAPTER

15

Body and Interior: Protecting Your Investment

In This Chapter

• • • • • • • • • • • •

- Checking and replacing lights and wiper blades

- How to clean your car, inside and out

- Which parts should you lubricate?

- How to touch up the paint

- The difference between polishing and waxing

Your car's appearance has absolutely no effect on how it runs or how dependable it is, but, strangely, its appearance may be the single most important consideration when determining its value.

Think about it: two cars, same year and model. One has faded paint and primer on the fenders. The other looks like someone just drove it off the showroom floor. You're drawn instantly to the more attractive car, even though the other car may be in better condition mechanically. In most cases, you'd be willing to pay more for the nicely waxed car regardless of which one runs better.

You're not alone. Most people feel the same way. That's why car dealers spend so much time and effort primping and polishing the cars on their lot. They want to dazzle you with that first impression. In this chapter, we'll look at how to keep your car looking nice through years of sun and weather. And remember: There's more to the body and interior than just appearance. You'll also learn how to take care of the hinges, weatherstripping, lights and lenses — the basic components that make up your car's body and interior.

Check the Lights and Wipers

Before you begin cleaning your car, you should take a few minutes and check the lights and wiper blades. If possible, have someone get inside the car and work the lights while you check them from the outside. Here are the items you should check:

- Headlights
- Parking lights (the first click on the headlight switch). Don't forget the license plate lights and side marker lights. They come on at the same time.
- Turn signals
- Brake lights
- Backup lights. They should come on automatically when you put the car in reverse.

You'll have to turn the key on to make the turn signals and backup lights work. You don't have to start the engine, just turn the key to the second click until the dash lights come on. That energizes the circuits to allow you to operate these lights.

If any light doesn't work, now is the time to fix it by replacing the necessary bulbs. In some cases, replacing the bulb is just a matter of removing a few screws. Other times it involves removing some plastic wing nuts in the trunk. Check your owner's manual for the proper procedure for your

CAUTION

Always apply the brakes when you put the car in reverse and make sure you put the gear selector back in park when you're finished.

car. It also should provide you with a listing of the bulb number for each of the lights on your car. Refer to that listing when purchasing new bulbs.

Most of the time, replacing the bulbs in the socket is just a matter of a simple push and twist. The little side-marker bulbs — usually a 194 bulb — just pull straight out. Be careful removing the bulb because old bulbs often break and can cause a serious cut. Use a rag to hold the bulb, and stop if the bulb starts to crack or break.

Now is also the time to check for cracks or damage to the lenses. If you see a damaged lens, order a new one. In most cases, these lenses won't be available through an aftermarket parts store, so you'll have to order them through the dealer. Sometimes you may be able to replace the lens yourself. If not, the procedure will warrant taking your car to the repair shop to have the lens replaced.

While you're checking the lights, don't forget the wiper blades and washer fluid. Replace the blades if they're torn or damaged. If they streak, try cleaning them with some mild detergent and a soft rag. If they still streak, you'll need to replace them. Most wiper blades have lived a full life after about six months. If you aren't comfortable with changing your wiper blades, take your car to your local gas station. Many stations will replace them for the price of the blades, without charging you additional labor. Once you're sure the lights and wipers are working properly, you're ready to begin washing your car.

Professional Cleaning

If your car is particularly dirty or the paint is faded — or maybe price just isn't an object — you may want to opt for a professional cleaning. This isn't a car wash we're talking about, though some car washes offer this service. This is a professional *detailing* — the same procedure car dealers use to make their cars look brand new. Detailing a car usually includes steam-cleaning the engine compartment, shampooing the carpeting and upholstery, machine-polishing the finish and basically making the car look just like it did the day it was driven off the showroom floor.

You'll find companies that detail cars in your phone book, under automotive detailing. Detailing a car can cost anywhere from $100 to $200 — a substantial amount for a car wash. But remember: A lot more goes on than just washing the car, and many people feel that a good detail job is well worth the price.

Cleaning the Car Yourself

If you're going to clean your car yourself, the best place to begin is the interior. That way you aren't dragging hoses and extension cords across the car's freshly cleaned paint. Open the doors, trunk and hood, and drag a trash can or trash bag over to the car. Start working your way through the piles of trash, throwing out old fast-food wrappers, soda bottles, paper towels, envelopes, candy wrappers, chicken bones and anything else you probably can do without.

Once you have all the large trash out of the way, remove the floor mats. Now you're ready to vacuum the interior. Use a shop vacuum if you have one. The dirt and stones embedded in the carpeting could damage a regular vacuum cleaner. Vacuum the carpeting, seats, door panels and dashboard. Don't forget under the seats and in the crevices where the seats and backs meet. Take a look at the doorjambs and fenderwells. These areas often trap leaves and seeds, which can lead to rust in the panels.

Then head outside and get the trunk, including the trunk lid flange along the weatherstripping. This is where you'll usually find a lot of leaves and seeds, depending on where you normally park your car. Do the same thing with the air inlets at the top of the engine firewall. Finally, if the floor mats are carpeted, vacuum them, too.

Once you have the big, loose stuff removed and vacuumed away, you're ready to clean the interior. If there are no real stains or caked-on mud, you probably can clean the interior using a couple of buckets and rags. Make up a light soap solution in one bucket and use that to clean the seats, door panels, console, steering column and dashboard. Follow it up by rinsing it with a clean, damp rag. In most cases, that should be all you need to clean the interior.

In severe cases, you may need to go beyond the basic cleaning. This could include shampooing the carpeting or scrubbing the seats. Make sure you use an appropriate cleaner for the seat material. If your seats are leather, you could ruin them with a harsh cleanser. Check with your local auto parts store. They should stock all types of upholstery cleaners for washing your car's interior.

Don't forget to wipe down the doorjambs, doorposts and the edges of the trunk and hood. These areas usually get very dirty, and most people don't clean them at all. This can make a big difference in how your car looks when you're finished.

Lubricate the Hinges and Weatherstripping

Once you've finished cleaning the interior, take a minute to lubricate the moving parts of the doors, trunk and hood. A few drops of oil on the door hinges and latches can make all the difference in keeping them working properly and preventing wear or damage.

Don't stop there: Get yourself a can of silicone spray and spray a little onto a clean rag. Then wipe that onto the weatherstripping around the doors, windows and trunk. That silicone will help prevent the seals from dry-rotting, and keep them in good shape for years longer.

Finally, a little dab of lithium grease on the hood stops and alignment blocks will help prevent the hood from squeaking or making noise when you drive over bumps. Most parts stores will have lithium grease in a small tube, which is more than enough to last for years. All you need is a little dab, once or twice a year. Once you have everything lubricated, close the hood, trunk and doors. You're ready to move on to cleaning the exterior.

Cleaning the Exterior

This is what most people think about when you talk about washing the car: the hose, soap and a rag, and getting really wet. Before you start hosing the rest of the car, take care of the tires because most whitewall cleaners recommend applying the cleaner to a dry tire. If you're not using a regular whitewall cleaner, a good household spray cleaner also will do a good job.

Spray the cleaner onto the dry whitewall and wait about 10 seconds. Then use a wet, soapy scrub brush to scrub the tire and whitewall. Once you finish scrubbing the tire, take a soapy rag or brush and clean the wheel or wheel cover. Finally, hose the tire off. Then you're ready to move on to the next tire.

While you're cleaning the tires, take a moment to spray off the wheel well. Dirt, sand and salt become caked on inside the wheel well and provide the perfect conditions for rust to take hold. A simple concentrated spray from a garden hose can be enough to loosen and remove that dirt — and keep your car lasting years longer.

Once you have the tires, wheels and wheel wells cleaned, you're ready to wash the rest of the car. There are dozens of cleaners on the market, but you can do a good job with a weak solution of dish detergent and a clean rag. You also may want to opt for one of the single-step, wash-and-wax solutions. These solutions work fine for making your car look good in the short term, but the wax they apply doesn't really protect the finish. It's there simply to make the car shiny for a few days. If you decide to use one of these all-in-one cleaners, follow the directions on the bottle for best results.

To wash your car the regular way, hose it off, starting with the roof. Once you have the roof wet, wash it thoroughly with the soapy rag. Then hose it off again. Continue on to the hood, trunk and, finally, the sides. Keep moving from one area to the next, until you have the whole car clean.

If you find tar or grease splattered along the bottom of the panels, there are special cleaners you can get at your local parts store to soften and remove it. Follow the directions on the can. Once you have the tar and grease removed, wash the area again with the soap solution.

If you aren't going to wax the car, finish up by wiping your car down with a damp chamois or a clean, damp towel. Wipe each area down using straight, even strokes, moving all the way across the panel. This will prevent the panel from becoming waterspotted.

Touching Up the Paint

Before you consider waxing the car, take a look around. Are there any paint chips or nicks that need to be repaired? Now is when you want to do that — after you've washed the dirt away, but before you put on a coat of wax. If you have any chips that need to be touched up, the first thing you'll need is a bottle of touch-up paint. This is a small bottle of paint that matches the paint on the car. It comes with its own touch-up brush.

Most parts stores have touch-up paint available. The trick is knowing the right color to buy. Say your car is blue. If you look in the application book, you'll probably find a half-dozen blues for your make and model. You may be able to eliminate a few just by their description, but some will sound — and look — pretty close.

There's a stamped metal tag under the hood of your car that provides all of the trim and paint information for it. It may be on the firewall or mounted to the radiator support. If you can't find it, check with your local repair shop. They should be able to help you find the color code for your car. Once you have the color code, it's a cinch to use that to determine the color for your car, using the application book at the parts store.

Never attempt to repair nicks or scratches in the paint in direct sunlight or on extremely hot or cold days. And always make sure the surface is completely dry before touching it up. To touch up the paint, first shake the touch-up paint bottle thoroughly. This will help provide you with the best match possible. Then, remove the lid and wipe the brush off to remove some of the paint. Too much paint will glob on or drip when you apply it.

NOTICE

Touch-up paint also is available in small spray cans. In general, that's for repairing larger areas and requires much more preparation than a basic touch-up. If the area you're trying to touch up is large enough to require a spray can, you might want to consider taking it to a body shop.

Next, touch the brush onto the nick. Don't brush, touch. Dab a little on and then leave it alone. If you need more paint to cover the nick, repeat the process: dip the brush, wipe it off and touch. Finish quickly and then leave it alone. Never go back and try to fix it up after the paint is in place. You'll just end up making it worse. If you need to add more paint, wait until the first application dries and then repeat the procedure the same way you did it the first time: dip, wipe, touch. That's all there is to touching up the paint.

Polishing the Finish

If your car's finish is in good shape, you'll probably be able to go right to waxing it without having to polish it up first. But if the paint is faded or damaged, the only way you may be able to get it to shine again is by using a polishing compound.

Polishing compound usually is a liquid or paste with mild abrasive particles. When you use the polish on the paint, the abrasive particles actually strip away the topmost layer of the paint to bring back the luster that the elements have faded. You can polish the car by hand or with a buffer. Polishing by hand is a lot of work. A buffer is somewhat easier, but it's risky. If you don't know what you're doing, you could easily polish through the paint.

To polish the car's finish, make sure the body is fairly cool and park it in the shade away from direct sunlight. Then start polishing a little area at a time. Apply the polish and rub it in, using a circular motion. As you rub, the faded paint will begin to lift off and reveal the original paint color underneath.

The trick to using a buffer with polishing compound is to keep the buffer moving. If you stop at any one place, you can be sure you'll burn through in no time. Be especially careful along edges and corners. They're the first places the paint is likely to burn away.

Once you have the car polished, you'll have to apply a good coat of wax to keep the shine. Because polishing the car removes the top layer and exposes the lower layers to the elements, if you don't wax it right away, it'll probably fade again in no time.

Waxing the Car

Many of today's cars come with a clear coat of paint. According to the manufacturers, these cars don't need to be waxed — the clear coat provides all the protection they need. That may be, but clear coat or not, nothing shines and protects a car's finish like a fresh coat of wax.

Today's waxes are very different from the waxes your father and grandfather used on their cars. Those hard waxes still are available, with names like Simonize and Blue Coral. They still provide excellent protection and a terrific shine. And they're still just as much work to apply.

But today there are dozens of new waxes available, designed with polymers and other space-age materials to provide a superior shine, while protecting your car's paint. There are even some waxes specifically colored to hide scratches and cracks in the finish. What's more, most of these new waxes are far easier to apply and polish off than the waxes of old. If you follow the directions on the can, these waxes provide a hard, durable shine without becoming a major production.

In most cases, there are four basic "tricks" to using today's waxes:

1 Make sure the car's body is relatively cool.

2 Apply the wax with the car in the shade, never in direct sunlight.

3 Work in a small amount of wax at a time, using a circular motion. Don't apply too much wax.

4 Let the wax dry to a dull, slightly opaque finish before polishing.

If you follow those simple directions, the excess wax will polish right off, leaving you with a deep, durable shine.

Protecting the Vinyl

One of the newest fads for protecting and cleaning your car is vinyl protectants. These products claim to provide protection for your dashboard, seats, door panels, vinyl roof and even the tires. Do they work? Yes, they do. They provide a solid level of protection for all the vinyl and rubber on your car.

The only problem is the finish. Most of these protectants create an unnaturally shiny finish wherever you use them. One look and you know something's been done to create this shine. Most of the time it won't wear off, so there's no going back once you've applied it. Some folks like that shiny look. The only way you'll know if you do is to try it, somewhere hidden, such as the bottom of the dashboard or the back of a seat. If you like the finish, use it to your heart's content.

A better way to protect your car's interior from sun damage — without the shiny finish — is to use one of those fold-up windshield covers when you park. You know the ones. You see them all over the parking lot, with cute sayings, slogans, ads or pictures on them. They block out the sunlight to protect the interior while your car is parked and prevent damage without creating an unnatural appearance. To protect and shine your tires, a little application of silicone will do nicely, again without creating an unnatural appearance.

Cleaning and protecting your car's appearance is easy, and there are hundreds of products designed to help you do just that. With a little care and a little elbow grease, you can keep your car looking like new for years to come.

CHAPTER

16

Driving Safer, Longer, Cheaper

In This Chapter

• • • • • • • • • • •

- How to improve your car's gas mileage

- How to drive to reduce wear and tear on your car

- How to drive in the snow

- What to do if you get stuck in the snow, mud or sand

- Preparing for a long trip

- Emergency items you should have onboard

It's no secret that proper maintenance will help keep your car in good running condition. And it also can improve your car's gas mileage and reduce your repair bills over time.

But what many people don't realize is that how you drive can be just as effective in improving your gas mileage, cutting repair costs and protecting your safety. Simple things, like pumping the brake pedal, can make a dramatic difference in certain repair costs over the life of your car. In this chapter, we'll explore some of the ways you can get more miles and fewer repair bills, while driving safer than ever before.

Improving Your Fuel Mileage

Traditional wisdom says you'll get your best gas mileage if you drive like you have a raw egg under the pedals. That's actually good advice. The object is to prevent sudden, harsh movements of either the gas or brake pedal. And there are a few others that, when used together, can make a real difference in the gas you use.

1. Avoid jackrabbit starts. Slow, gentle accelerations provide the best gas mileage. Quick accelerations dump extra gas into the engine to get the car moving.

2. Anticipate your stops. If the light turned red up the road, let off the gas now. Let the car coast a while. You may not even have to touch the brakes before the light changes, and you can start moving again.

3. Drive during cooler times of the day in the summer. The air is denser when the temperature is cooler, so you can get more power and better mileage from your engine.

4. Don't let the car idle. Those long warm-ups in the morning may make your drive more comfortable for a few minutes, but they waste a lot of gas.

5. Combine your trips. Your car uses more gas when the engine is cold than when it's hot. If you combine your errands, the engine warms up and stays that way through the entire trip, using less gas overall.

6. Use the air conditioning. A few years back the advice was the opposite: Turn the air off and open the windows. But today's air conditioners are more efficient than a few years ago, and they create less drag on the engine than driving with the windows open.

7. Lighten the load. Don't haul extra weight in the vehicle. A heavier vehicle uses more gasoline.

8. Maintain the recommended air pressure in your tires. Low pressure reduces fuel economy and can cause damage to the tires.

9. Keep the air filter clean. Restricted filters can substantially reduce fuel economy and increase exhaust emissions.

10. Drive the speed limit.

Driving to Reduce Vehicle Wear

Believe it or not, how you drive can have a major impact on your repair bills. For example, something as simple as easing up on the gas pedal at just the right moment can determine whether your transmission lasts just a few years or the life of the car.

Here are a few tips that could make a difference to your car and your wallet:

1. No jackrabbit starts. Just like it improves gas mileage, easy acceleration puts less strain on the various powertrain components and can help them last longer.

2. Ease off the gas just before shifts. Pay attention to when the transmission shifts and learn to ease up on the gas just before them. This takes the load off the transmission during the shifts, so the clutches and bands have less stress and tend to last longer.

3. Pump the brakes. Each time you release the brake pedal, the brakes get a moment to cool off. This can prevent the brakes from overheating and keeps them working longer.

4. One foot, two pedals. Never use your left foot to apply the brakes. Use the right foot for the gas and the brakes. Left-footed drivers tend to rest their foot on the brake pedal. This prevents the brakes from releasing all the way, so they burn up in no time.

5. Use the brakes, not the clutch. If you have a manual transmission, avoid the temptation to use the clutch to slow the car. A set of brakes costs maybe a third of the price of a clutch. Which would you rather pay for?

6. Don't run the tank dry. When the gas gets below a quarter of a tank, it tends to slosh around more. The fuel pump then starts sucking air, which can reduce its useful life.

7. Don't drive over something you can avoid. You wouldn't believe the damage that a simple plastic bag can cause to your car. Not to mention potholes, manhole covers, branches and so on. When possible, avoid them altogether.

How to Drive in Snow

The key to driving in snow is inertia. You probably remember this from back in middle school: A body at rest tends to remain at rest; a body in motion tends to remain in motion. So how do you take advantage of Sir Isaac Newton's wisdom?

1. Accelerate and decelerate slowly. Apply the gas slowly to accelerate. Don't try to get moving in a hurry. And take time to slow down for a stoplight. Remember: It's going to take longer to slow down on icy roads.

2. Drive slowly. Everything's going to take longer on snow-covered roads. Accelerating, stopping, turning — nothing will happen as quickly as on dry pavement. Give yourself time to maneuver by driving slowly.

3. Pump the brakes. Snow and ice can easily break the friction between the road and the tires, causing them to lock up. Pumping the brakes allows the wheels to begin turning again, so you can regain control of the car and slow it gently.

4. Don't stop if you can avoid it. Remember: A body at rest tends to stay at rest. There's a big difference in the amount of inertia it takes to start moving from a full stop and how much it takes to get moving while still rolling. If you can slow down enough to keep rolling until the light changes, do it.

5. Don't power up hills. Applying extra gas on snow-covered roads just starts your wheels spinning. Try to get a little inertia going before you reach the hill and let that inertia carry you to the top.

6. Don't stop going up a hill. There's nothing worse than trying to get moving up a hill on an icy road. Get some inertia going on flat roadway before you take on the hill. Then when the light changes, you can get moving and let the inertia carry you over the hill.

7. Stay home. If you really don't have to go out, don't. Even if you can drive well in the snow, not everyone else can. Don't tempt fate: If you don't have somewhere you have to be, watch the snow from indoors.

If You're Stuck in the Snow, Mud or Sand

The worst thing you can do if your car gets stuck in the snow, mud or sand is rev the engine and spin the wheels. All you'll do is bury the wheels even deeper and make it that much harder to get free. But in many cases, spinning the wheels will damage or even destroy your transmission. And you can bet that'll cost a lot more than calling for a tow truck.

The real trick to getting out of the snow, mud or sand is to rock the car back and forth, until the car's momentum is strong enough to carry it out. Here's how:

Make sure the wheels stop turning completely before shifting the transmission.

- Put the transmission in low gear and give the engine a little gas.
- Once the car stops moving forward — even if it's only a few inches — release the gas and apply the brakes.
- Shift into reverse and give the car a little gas. If all goes well, it'll move just a little farther than it did the first time.
- Once the car stops moving backward, release the gas and apply the brakes. Repeat the procedure — forward, backward, forward, backward. Each time you should move a little farther, until you get enough momentum to drive the car right out of the snow (or mud or sand). And don't discount the power of a strong back. A few people pushing together can make all the difference in helping you break free.

Preparing for a Long Trip

If you're like most people, one of your biggest fears when preparing for a road trip is being at the mercy of a shop where they know you're from out of town. Maybe they'll take advantage of you, and maybe they won't, but who needs that aggravation when they're on vacation?

To avoid trouble on the road, there are a few things you can do:

Have your car serviced a few weeks before leaving on vacation. Not a few *days* — a few *weeks*. That way, if you run into any problems with the work, you're still home to have it taken care of by your regular repair shop, instead of on the road, dealing with strangers.

1. Have your car serviced. Is your car coming due for any maintenance work? Now is the time to have that done, even if it's a little early. Lube, oil and filter, tire rotation, tune-up — whatever is getting close. Do it now to make sure everything is up to date.

2. Have your car inspected, whether it's due for a state inspection or not. Have them check the lights, tires, brakes, suspension and steering, exhaust and anything else that would be checked for a normal safety inspection.

3. Ask to have your car checked over for a trip. The technician will examine the belts, hoses, fluid levels and basically anything that can wear, leak or burn. He'll look for unusual conditions such as vibrations or noises that indicate a problem that could get you stuck.

4. Make sure the air conditioning is working properly. If it doesn't seem to be cooling right, have it looked at now. Remember: You're going to be spending a lot of time in your car, so you want to be comfortable.

5. Check the tire pressure, including the spare, and make sure the jack is in good working order.

6. Hide some emergency cash in your car — or traveler's checks or a credit card. That way, you're sure to have some money on hand for an emergency situation.

7. Get current maps for the area where you're going to be traveling. Your local AAA office can help you with that. Or look into one of the new satellite navigational devices available.

Emergency Items You Should Have

When it comes to emergency items you should always have on hand, there's one thing you can be sure of: No matter how much stuff you pack into your car, the first time you have an emergency, you probably won't have what you need. But that's no reason to leave yourself completely unprepared. Here's a basic list of emergency items that you should try to keep on hand in case of an emergency.

Jack and Spare Tire — Don't forget to check the air pressure in your spare once in awhile.

Lug Wrench — Lug wrenches make it easy to loosen and tighten the lug nuts. They come in different sizes, so make sure the one you get fits your car's lug nuts.

Wheel Chocks — These are just triangular pieces of wood or strong plastic that you can wedge under the wheels to keep them from rolling — and an important safety item when you're changing a tire.

Flashlight — If possible, get yourself one that will stand freely and allow you to aim the light where you're working. If it has a warning blinker built in, so much the better. And don't forget to replace the batteries once in awhile: Change them the same time you change the battery in your home smoke detector.

Triangular Reflectors — Whether you're the one who's stuck or you want to help someone else by the side of the road, reflectors or highway light sticks can help prevent a tragic accident.

WARNING

If your car came with one of those "space saver" spares that has to be inflated when you need it, get rid of it. They're unsafe. Replace it with a normal spare tire or one of the smaller, inflated space-saving spares.

Tip Provided by
Ed Welsh
AAA Utica and Central New York

Jumper Cables – Spend a few extra dollars here and get a decent set: at least 6-gauge copper wire for a 12-foot set and good, sturdy clamps. Forget about those battery chargers that plug into your cigarette lighter. They only work if you have about a week to wait.

Tool Kit – With these basic items: pliers, screwdrivers, socket set, duct tape, electrical tape, assorted hose clamps, knife, assorted fuses, assorted bulbs, mechanic's wire.

Fire Extinguisher – A good, dry-chemical, multipurpose fire extinguisher will last for years and costs only a few dollars.

Sand – If it snows in your area, there's nothing like simple construction sand to provide traction on ice-covered roads. A 50-pound bag costs only a few dollars and should last many years. Fill an old laundry detergent bottle with the sand and slip it under your seat. That way it'll be right there when you need it, and you won't have to open the trunk while standing in the middle of the road.

Extra Oil and Water – Sometimes a gallon of plain water or a quart of oil can be the difference between getting home or getting stuck. Of course, if it gets cold in your area, a gallon of premixed antifreeze and water will keep even better, and won't freeze in your trunk.

$20 – or $50 or $100 or whatever you're likely to need. Take some cash, fold it up and tuck it away in a nice, safe place. If your wallet gets stolen, that emergency cash might be just what you need for a meal, a tank of gas, a bridge toll or a room for the night.

Cell Phone – The most valuable emergency tool you can keep on hand is a cell phone. With a cell phone, you never have to worry about what to do when your car breaks down. Police, fire, ambulance and the AAA emergency road service are always right at your fingertips.

Personal Safety Items

First Aid Kit – Nothing too fancy, just a simple little kit with adhesive bandages, a few aspirin, a little ointment, maybe a pair of tweezers. You can get one from your local pharmacy for just a few dollars.

Space Blanket – If you're in an area where the weather gets cold, a space blanket is a great item to keep on hand. This is a thin, mylar blanket designed to reflect most of your body heat. It's so thin that a full-size blanket folds into a tiny packet small enough to fit into your glove compartment.

Medicines – Are you, or any member of your family, on prescription medication? It wouldn't be a bad idea to take a couple of days worth of pills and make up a little emergency kit to keep in your glove compartment in case you find yourself away from home overnight.

And there are other items you may want to keep on hand, depending on your personal skills and desires, and where you live — like snow chains, a shovel and a more complete tool kit.

- If you usually drive in a cold climate, you may want to include some extra warm clothing, a hat and some gloves.
- If you usually drive in a more temperate area, you may be more interested in sunscreen, sunglasses and insect repellant.
- And if you often find yourself driving through a desert, don't forget to keep some drinking water on hand . . . just in case.

What you include is limited only by your imagination, your desire to be prepared and the size of your trunk.

CHAPTER

17

When Your Car Needs Repairs

In This Chapter

• • • • • • • • • • • •

- Six steps for choosing the right repair facility

- Introducing AAA's Approved Auto Repair Program

- Getting the best service from your repair facility

- How to explain your car's problem to a repair technician

- Why you should expect to pay for diagnosis

One day you'll be forced to look for a repair shop. Whether it's for something as simple as a flat tire or as complicated as an engine overhaul, someday your car's going to let you down. The key to having your car repaired properly — and at the right price — is a combination of finding a quality repair facility and having good communication with the service technician.

Both are equally important. If the repair facility isn't a good one, they may not be able to give you the repairs you want at the price you should be paying. And if you don't communicate your problem clearly with the shop personnel, there's a good chance you won't be satisfied with the repairs.

In this chapter, we'll show you how to choose a quality repair facility that's staffed by expert personnel. Then we'll discuss how to get the repairs you want, by teaching you how to explain your problem and to make sure the technician knows what you're looking for.

Choosing a Repair Facility

The first step in having your car repaired is finding a good repair shop. But how do you choose? With all of the different repair centers out there, how do you select one that will provide dependable, honest service at a reasonable price?

Tough call. Because, while there are some key elements that indicate a good repair center, they're by no means a sure thing. Some of the worst shops hide that fact behind a façade that projects an image of integrity and competence — at least, on the surface — while some of the best ones seem to violate all the rules for image. It's up to you to look a little deeper to make sure you're choosing a quality repair center.

Price is also a double-edged sword. The lowest price may reflect low overhead or cheap parts. Price is important but not the best factor to use when selecting a repair facility. If you get an estimate that is substantially higher or lower than other shops in the area, be wary.

Here's a list of some clues you can look for, some telltale signs that will help you decide whether to trust a shop with your car. But remember: Don't just use one or two of these tips as your guide. Make sure the shop you choose passes several of these criteria before you give them your business and your trust.

Recommendation — The first thing most people do when looking for a new shop is to ask for recommendations. Talk to friends, family, co-workers — anyone whose opinion you trust. Find out where they take their cars and ask about their experiences, the quality of work, dependability and price. Once you've narrowed your choice down to a few shops, you're ready to move on to the next step.

Reputation – Check with the Better Business Bureau and local consumer agencies. See if there are any reports of problems or unresolved disputes. Find out how long the shop has been in business. Once you've chosen a shop that seems acceptable, you're ready to pay them a visit.

Appearance – Don't expect crystal chandeliers and thick pile carpeting: This is a repair shop, not a fine restaurant. But it should be neat and clean. There's no reason you should see old parts or used tires piled up out front. The waiting room and customer service areas should be clean and well-lighted, and service writers should offer a friendly greeting and a smile.

Certification – Look around the waiting room for technician certifications. While no guarantee of competence, these certifications do indicate a certain level of professionalism and pride in accomplishment. Look for these certifications:

ASE – The National Institute for Automotive Service Excellence certifies automotive professionals in 42 separate categories. ASE is the gold standard for technicians. If they don't have ASE certifications, chances are they aren't in it for the long haul.

State Inspection – Most states require certification for safety or emission repairs. These certifications show that the technician passed the necessary examinations to prove competence in these specific areas.

MACS or IMACA – Air conditioning specialty certifications, allowing technicians to service A/C refrigeration systems.

ATRA or ATSG – Automatic transmission repair certifications.

These are just the major certification programs. You may find other certificates indicating training from such organizations as EAST, CAAT, and individual parts and automobile manufacturers. Each one lends that much more credibility to the technician's claim of competence.

Equipment – Ask for a quick tour of the shop. Any good shop will be equipped to handle the repair services it offers. This should include lifts, jacks, alignment equipment, a wheel balancer, A/C recovery and recharging equipment, brake drum and rotor lathes, engine analyzers, and various handheld diagnostic and repair equipment. Most good shops also will have some level of parts inventory, including hoses, belts, ignition, brakes, batteries, bulbs and other basic items.

Warranty – A spoken warranty, like an oral contract, isn't worth the paper it's printed on. Any decent shop should have its warranty information printed on its repair orders or on the wall for all to see. Twelve months or 12,000 miles is fairly standard. If you don't see it posted on the wall or on the repair order, ask for the details of the warranty – in writing.

If a shop meets minimum standards on these six basic criteria, it's probably safe to trust them with your car.

AAA/CAA's Approved Auto Repair Program

AAA/CAA's Approved Auto Repair program assists its members in finding reputable repair facilities that perform quality work. This network of 6,800 repair facilities across North America provides valuable assistance to AAA and CAA members.

As a AAA or CAA member, you're entitled to these benefits when you take your car to an AAR facility for service:

Safety and Maintenance Inspection — At your request, you can have your car inspected at no charge, while having any other paid service performed.

Written Estimate — You can ask for a written estimate of all work necessary for your car; state and local regulations take precedence regarding repair cost notification.

Warranty — All work will be warranted for a minimum of 12 months or 12,000 miles — whichever comes first — on parts and labor, unless otherwise noted on the repair order.

Returned Parts — You can request that all replaced parts be returned to you for inspection, unless the parts must be returned to the manufacturer for warranty or exchange.

Dispute Resolution — AAA will investigate any dispute between the AAA member and the approved facility. The facility will abide by AAA's decision in the resolution of any dispute. As a member, you aren't bound by AAA's decision and may seek recourse through other avenues.

Any automotive repair center that meets and maintains AAA/CAA's standards and that is willing to abide by the terms of the program can become an Approved Auto Repair facility. Each approved facility undergoes an extensive review by AAA in these areas:

- Customer Service
- Facility Appearance
- Staff Qualifications and Training
- Community Reputation
- Insurance
- Financial Stability
- General Equipment

AAA approved facilities agree to perform a safety/maintenance inspection with any service or repair when asked by the AAA member; provide a minimum 12-month, 12,000 mile repair warranty on parts and labor; abide by AAA/CAA's final decision in resolving service complaints; take full responsibility for vehicle repairs, even when subletting a portion of those repairs.

Additionally, the Approved Auto Repair facility provides service in the areas of engine performance, brakes, electrical systems, minor repairs on engines. The facility may also service tires, steering and suspension systems, heating and air conditioning systems, manual or automatic transmissions, differential and axle and major repairs on engines.

Getting the Best Service

Regardless of a shop's overall quality and capability, you can be sure there's a wide variety in the quality of service different customers receive. That's not to suggest anyone's getting cheated. But no one will deny that people are more willing to go that extra mile for someone they really like.

So how do you work your way onto the A-list? Actually, it's easier than you might think. Remember that auto technicians and shop personnel are people just like you. They want to be liked and respected, and they're usually quick to reciprocate. Here are a few things to remember to help get the best a shop has to offer:

Be Friendly — Don't just walk in the door and throw your keys on the counter. Offer a smile and a greeting. Get to know the service writers and key personnel by name, and wish them a good morning. While you're waiting for your car, make small talk. Act like a friend. In most cases, it won't take long before you actually become one.

Find a Good Shop and Stick with It — Don't jump around from place to place. Find a shop that you can trust and use them all the time. Regular customers get first priority in most shops. That's just good business on the shop's part: to take care of their regulars first. The trick (and it's not such a difficult one) is to become one of the regulars.

Give Them the First Chance — Nothing annoys a repair shop more than seeing someone else's parts or lube stickers on your car. Oil changes, exhaust and brake jobs are the "gravy" — the high-profit, easy-to-handle, never-have-a-problem repairs — for the shop. If you give those jobs away, you can bet you won't make the top of the A-list. If you aren't sure whether your regular shop handles a certain type of repair, ask. They'll be happy to tell you whether they can help you with your problem. And if not, they may be able to direct you to someone who can — often for far less than you'd pay without their recommendation.

Be Empathetic — Auto repair is a difficult, demanding occupation. Recent studies indicate today's technicians have to be familiar with over a half-million pages of technical information to do their jobs. That's a lot of data to stay on top of. Make sure *they* know that *you* know. When you do have a problem that involves straight diagnostic time, show that you understand their dilemma. "Just do your best" shows that you trust them to do the job.

Talking to Your Technician

The success of any repair procedure often hinges on the first few minutes when you drop the car off, because that's when you explain the problem to the shop personnel. A poor or incomplete explanation can leave the technician grasping at straws. A good one can send the technician right to the source of the problem.

The thing to remember is that there's a big difference between *explaining* the problem and *diagnosing* it. No one's expecting you to know whether your problem is in the transmission or the computer system. That's a diagnosis.

But "in cold weather, the engine seems to rev up really high when the transmission shifts from first to second gear until it warms up" — now *that's* an explanation. It covers all the details the technician needs to know to duplicate the problem and make an accurate diagnosis.

In this section, you'll learn how to explain an automotive problem. You'll find out what the technician needs to know, what to say — and what *not* to say — by following these *five simple rules:*

Rule 1: Don't Expect Maintenance to Fix a Problem

You hear it in nearly every repair shop, almost any day of the week: "Just tune it up," or, "Service the transmission. I think it's due."

That would be great, if they were simply asking for maintenance. But all too often the person asking this is attempting to repair a problem. The customer hopes that during the tune-up — or transmission service or whatever — the technician will replace the component causing the problem, thereby fixing the problem without spending money for diagnosis. Don't count on it.

The problem is, years ago it worked. Back then a tune-up involved replacing the better part of the ignition system and checking the rest of it. It also included a number of filters, several adjustments and even cleaning out the passages inside the carburetor. Of course, a tune-up fixed performance problems: There wasn't much left to *cause* a problem.

But today things are different. Ignition systems are electronic, and adjustments are computer-controlled. The spark is hotter, fuels are cleaner, and the fuel system is sealed. So today's tune-up has less chance of repairing a problem. It still needs to be done, but chances are it won't fix anything.

The point is, if you have a driveability problem, say so. Tell the shop exactly what's happening and when. Let them know what seems different. Now is not the time to hold back. Be honest and thorough in your description. That's the best chance you'll have of getting your car repaired properly.

Of course, the car still will need to be tuned, the wheels aligned and the transmission serviced. But they're maintenance items, not repair items. Never count on a maintenance item to fix a problem. Just explain the problem, and let the shop do its job.

Rule 2: Explain the Problem, Don't Diagnose It

The worst thing you can do when you have a problem with your car is to tell the shop what to do. But every day, customers come into repair shops and say things like:

- *Check the charging system.*
- *Give it an alignment.*
- *Replace the valve cover gaskets.*

So the repair shop performs the work the customer asked for, returns the car, and the problem is still there. It's not that the shop was incompetent: They just did what they were asked to do. What's worse, the repair the customer asked for may not have been necessary at all. For example, the customer who asked for the charging system check may have had a bad starter. Or maybe there was a short, causing the battery to go dead. Either way, checking the charging system probably wouldn't have revealed the problem.

But if the technician had known the battery was going dead, he'd have checked the battery and the charging system. When nothing showed up, he'd move on to checking for a short in the system. Sure, it would have cost the customer something for the checks, but at least the car would have gotten fixed.

The person who asked for an alignment may have had a vibration at 55 mph. Alignment won't cause that problem. More likely, a wheel was out of balance. But since the shop didn't know about the problem, the technician didn't know what to look for. So they performed an alignment, and the problem was still there. The best way to avoid this is to explain the problem, not try to diagnose it yourself.

- Instead of asking to have the charging system checked, say, *The battery keeps going dead. I have to have it jumped to get the engine to start.*
- Instead of asking for an alignment, say, *The car seems to vibrate at about 55 mph. You can feel it in the steering.*

By explaining the problem instead of trying to diagnose it, you stand a far better chance of having your car repaired properly.

Rule 3: Provide the Details

Explaining a problem clearly depends on being able to give the repair shop a clear picture of exactly what's happening, so they can reproduce that problem for themselves. This often involves more that just "it doesn't run right." In many cases, it requires being able to identify separate conditions of the complaint that we'll call the four W's:

What is the car doing? This is where you explain the specifics of the complaint. Is it running rough? Is it hard to start? Is there a noise? Poor gas mileage? A vibration? Any warning lights come on? Whatever you noticed that made you think there was a problem, this is where you need to explain it.

When does the problem occur? Does it happen only when you start it up, after it's been sitting awhile? After it's been running a few minutes or a few miles? Immediately after shutting the engine off?

What was the **weather** like? Does the problem occur all the time, or is it linked to the weather? Was it hot or cold? Raining or dry?

The problem occurs **while** . . . Does the problem only occur while idling? On hard throttle or cruise? While accelerating or decelerating? Only while making a hard turn?

A good description of a problem will include all of these four W's. Here are a couple of good examples: *My car seems to run rough whenever it's raining. I notice it most at idle, particularly after it's been running for a few minutes.* Or, *My car makes a loud noise from the front on the passenger's side during hard right turns. It doesn't seem to matter how long I've been driving or whether it's cold or hot out.*

Pay attention to these details when the problem occurs so you'll be able to explain them later. It's not enough to just know that the car hesitates in the morning. What's important is that it acts up only after you've driven about half a mile but seems to go away after a couple miles.

That kind of detail in the explanation may be all that's necessary to turn a real problem into a simple diagnosis for your repair shop. Remember: Details will help the discussion, and not only will that save you money, it could easily make the difference between a comeback and a single success-ful visit to the repair shop.

Rule 4: Avoid Technical Jargon

As with every other business in the world today, auto repair has its own language. Words like *hesitation* and *misfire* have their own very specific meanings, and they evoke a very specific set of conditions to technicians.

Problems arise when consumers try to use these terms to describe the problems with their cars. Unless you've spent years working on cars, those words probably won't mean the same thing to you as they would to a technician.

In fact, the technician doesn't necessarily know that you're using the word to mean something else. So when you talk about a hesitation, the shop checks the car for a hesitation — using the definition that technicians understand. If you had something different in mind, they end up wasting time and your money looking for a problem that isn't there.

To avoid that, use common terms. Don't be ashamed to say, "The car seems to hiccup repeatedly at about 40 mph." Sure, the service writer and technician may have a good laugh — probably *with* you, not *at* you. And then the technician will go out and find the problem in the most efficient manner because your description will identify the complaint clearly to anyone who listens. To make sure you and the shop understand one another, avoid jargon. Always explain the problem in the simplest language possible.

Rule 5: When Possible, Demonstrate the Problem

No matter how clearly or carefully you describe a problem, someone's going to misunderstand. It's not that they're being deliberately obtuse, it's just that words have different meanings for different people. For example, suppose someone told you they heard a squealing noise coming from the front of their car. Immediately, your mind would recall a noise you once heard that you'd describe as a squeal. That noise may not even be remotely similar to the noise the other person heard, even though the word "squeal" may have been a perfectly accurate description of both sounds.

So how do you deal with this disparity between description and memory? Show them the problem. Ask the service writer or technician to come out to the car with you and let them hear the problem for themselves. Or get them to drive the car with you, to feel the steering problem . . . or the transmission problem . . . or whatever the problem is that you're complaining about.

That way you take all of the misunderstanding out of the equation. Once they've heard, felt or seen the problem, there's no chance of, *It didn't do it for me*, or, *I thought you were talking about something else*"; cropping up. Of course, there will be those times when you can't show them the problem, such as one that goes away after you drive the car for a few miles. That type of problem may be impossible to demonstrate because by the time you reach the shop, it's gone.

In that case you'll have to leave the car overnight, so it'll have time to cool down and the problem can show up. And that's where you'll have to rely on your ability to describe the problem. Refer to the four W's of describing a problem — what, when, weather and while — and do your best. But whenever possible, show them the problem. Once they've experienced the problem for themselves, you have a far better chance of getting your car fixed right.

Expect to Pay for Diagnosis

Many people are upset when they find out they have to pay for diagnostic time. They expect to pay for the actual repairs, but they figure the diagnostic time should be included.

"Why should I pay for diagnostic time? That didn't fix anything," is what they often say. But the fact is, without the diagnosis, there'd be no way to determine what needed to be repaired.

When a doctor prescribes diagnostic testing, you expect to pay for that. Even insurance companies — notoriously stingy when it comes to paying claims — expect to pay for diagnostic procedures. Even if the tests don't reveal anything wrong, they still pay. In many cases, those diagnostic tests cost far more than the actual treatment. That's because the equipment needed for diagnosis often is far more complex — and costly — than the equipment needed for treatment.

The same is true for automotive diagnosis. For example, suppose your car's *Check Engine* light comes on. The problem turns out to be a bad MAP sensor hose. The repair is simply a matter of replacing the hose. That's the easy part: Anyone can do that. But finding that hose problem amidst the web of wires, sensors and hoses — *that's* the hard part. It usually involves connecting an expensive piece of equipment called a *scan tool* to the computer system.

This scan tool enables the technician to check for codes and read through sensor operation — basically letting the tech spy on the computer signals. The technician evaluates all the information based on the electrical signals and diagnostic codes, and then narrows the problem down to find the damaged hose.

Which part of the repair was more involved: identifying and isolating the problem, or replacing the hose? Which part required more equipment? More knowledge? More time?

Obviously the diagnosis is a large part of the repair and requires more skill, equipment and time. And that's why you should expect to see diagnostic time on your repair bill. It's a legitimate charge and should be treated as such.

CHAPTER
18

Buying a Used Car

In This Chapter

• • • • • • • • • • •

- How to determine the value of the car you're looking at

- How to learn its history

- Preliminary checks you should make

- Why you should have it checked by a repair shop and what to expect from them

- Should you buy an extended warranty?

Few tasks relating to your car are more harrowing than buying it — particularly if you're buying a used car. During this process, you're asked to hand over a relatively large sum of money, based on a superficial examination, limited drive time and the word of someone who sells used cars for a living. Not the most encouraging set of circumstances.

What's more, there's a whole industry of professionals whose primary occupation is to turn a rusted, hulking deathtrap-on-wheels into something that appears to be good transportation. A little sawdust to quiet up a noisy differential, a cheap paint job to hide the rust, a quick mileage adjustment, a thorough cleanup and just like that, trash becomes cash — *your* cash.

So how do you keep from being taken for a ride? Unfortunately, there are no guarantees. Even the sharpest car buyer sometimes gets stuck. But there are ways to improve your chances and reduce the likelihood of getting a lemon. In this chapter, we'll give you a few tips on how to spot deals that really *are* just too good to be true. And we'll help you learn to recognize a real deal when you see it.

Know the Value

Before you can make an intelligent decision on any used car purchase, you need to know what it's worth, because a good deal doesn't automatically mean the car doesn't need any repair work. It means that the car can be repaired to like-new condition and that the total cost for the car and the repairs is less than the car's appraised value.

For example, say you're looking at two cars, both worth about $5,000 in good condition. One runs good, but a thorough examination reveals that it needs about $1,000 in repairs to the brakes, exhaust, ignition — that sort of thing. The asking price on the car is $4,500. When you road-tested the second car, it wouldn't shift. Chances are the transmission will need to be rebuilt. A thorough examination reveals the rest of the car to be in good condition.

Should you avoid the second car? Not necessarily: It depends on the asking price and the cost of rebuilding the transmission. For example, suppose the asking price for the car were $2,500. If the transmission could be rebuilt for $1,500, that would leave you with a total cost of $4,000 — a thousand below its value and $1,500 below the cost of the other car.

What's more, if you buy and repair the second car, you'll have a car with a rebuilt transmission and a warranty, instead of a transmission that's still waiting to fail. If everything else looks good, the second car probably is the better deal.

How can you find the car's value? The *Kelley Blue Book*® and N.A.D.A. Appraisal Guides have been the standard for car values for years. And now you can check the *Blue Book* or *N.A.D.A.* appraised value on the web at www.kbb.com or nadaguides.com. Or enter the car's information, including model, mileage, approximate condition and accessories. You'll get the car's average value, adjusted for its condition and your region. With the car's average value, the asking price and the estimate of repairs, you can make an informed decision about which car is a good deal. You can use this information to help decide what car to buy or how much to ask for a car you may be selling. Check your local AAA website for more information about used cars.

Check the History

You check the car over, and everything looks good. No obvious damage, everything works and runs fine, and the mileage is reasonable. Sounds like a done deal, right? Maybe. Maybe not. Remember: There are all sorts of ways to hide problems in a car. A quick paint job, a thorough cleaning, roll the odometer back a few thousand miles and who's to know?

But you can find out that information with a small investment and an Internet connection. For just $20 for an unlimited number of searches, you can check on damage records, ownership records, inspection records and anything that's ever been recorded about the car you're looking at.

Just go to aaa.com to request a vehicle history report, using the vehicle identification number, the VIN, of the car you're looking at. You'll receive a complete listing of any records of damage or repairs recorded for the car you're looking at. A vehicle history report can't be wiped away by all the paint and polish in the world. It's a great way to be sure the car you're looking at is everything it appears to be.

Mileage Matters

One of the first checks you should make when looking at a used car is the mileage, because the number on the odometer will determine what you should be looking for while checking the rest of the car. For example, say you're looking at a car with just 5,000 miles on the odometer. That's practically new. Your next step would be to try to confirm that mileage by looking at some of the car's "tells."

Since you already have the door open, start with the interior. Check the pedal pads, carpeting, driver's seat and armrests. You shouldn't see any wear on any of them. If any of these areas show signs of wear, suspect the mileage of being tampered with.

Next, check the doorjamb for any lube stickers that would contradict the mileage. Also look in the glove compartment for receipts or service records — anything that might indicate the mileage was altered. Check the tires. With 5,000 miles, the tires should be fairly new, but not brand new. Maybe $^{10}/_{32}$ of an inch tread. Examine the wheels or rims for marks from wheel weights. If you see additional weight marks, it indicates the tire has been rebalanced. While that's possible, it's not likely with so few miles.

OK, you've checked the "tells," and you're convinced the mileage is genuine. Now you start to examine the body and notice the car has just been completely repainted. "Oh, that's just because of parking lot nicks and scratches," the salesperson tells you. Watch out: Nobody repaints an entire car for parking lot nicks. They might repaint the sides, but that's about it. Chances are that car was hit, and hit hard. In fact, that's probably why it's for sale. A body shop bought the car for fill-in work when things got slow. Once it was fixed, they put it up for sale.

On the other hand, on an *older* car with low mileage, a full paint job might be more reasonable. The old paint may have faded over the years, even though the car wasn't driven all that much. In that case, you'll have to look deeper to determine whether it was just a paint job or something more.

On an exceptionally low-mileage car, you'll want to concentrate more on looking for accident or water damage and less on wear. Let's face it, not much is going to wear in 5,000 miles. On the other hand, if the miles are higher, you'll want to spend more time looking for mechanical wear. The important thing to remember is to use the car's mileage to direct your examination.

Examine the Car Thoroughly

The next step in checking a used car is to examine the car thoroughly. Here's a list of things you should be looking for:

Ownership — Whether you do it now or later is up to you, but before you hand over one dime, make sure the person you're dealing with has the right to sell the car. Compare the VIN on the car with the one on the paperwork. If the numbers don't match, pass.

Body Damage — Examine the car carefully for any signs of repaired body damage. Here are some of the clues of a previous hit:

- Paint mismatches, in color or finish quality
- Paint on the moldings, door handles, windows or anywhere it doesn't belong. Don't forget to check the doorjambs and under the hood and trunk lid for overspray.

TECH TIP One good way to find plastic filler in a car's body panel is with one of those kid's magnets available from any toy store. Hold the magnet against the suspect panel and see if it attracts anything. Any more than about one-eighth of an inch of plastic will prevent the magnet from being pulled toward the panel.

- Missing, mismatched or obviously new moldings
- Cracks between the doors, hood and trunk that are wider or closer than others that could indicate prior body damage

Water Leaks — Check the trunk and passenger compartment for wetness, stains or a severe musty smell. Any of these conditions could indicate a water leak.

Mechanical Condition — This is where you check for any obvious mechanical problems:

- Under the hood, check for signs of improper maintenance: worn belts, hard or mushy hoses, dirty battery cable ends, low fluid levels or anything that indicates the car hasn't received the required maintenance.
- Open the oil fill cap and look for signs of foam or caked-on deposits. Either of these conditions could indicate missed oil changes or an engine problem.
- Look for any obvious damage: broken or frayed wires, cracked hoses, missing components or anything that just doesn't look right.
- If the transmission has a dipstick, pull it out and check the fluid. Look at it and give it a sniff. If it's obviously burnt, suspect a transmission problem.
- Look for signs of recent problems. Freshly replaced components could indicate someone was trying to fix a problem. This doesn't necessarily indicate an ongoing problem, but it's something you should address with a professional technician.
- Check the tailpipe. Heavy black soot could indicate a performance problem.
- Turn the key on, engine off. Check the warning lights on the dash. All of the lights — except the temperature light — should come on. If the car has gauges instead of lights, the gauges should indicate properly. For example, with the key on, engine off, oil pressure should read zero PSI.
- Start the engine. It should start fairly quickly, with no real problems or unusual noises. During the start-up, the temperature light should come on and go out once you release the key.
- Check the warning lights and gauges with the engine running. Lights should go out immediately, and the gauges should register properly.
- See how the engine feels when it's running. It should be reasonably smooth, without any roughness or shake.
- With the engine running, listen for noises in the engine compartment. Tapping, banging, whirring or squealing noises could indicate a simple adjustment or could be signs of a major problem.

IMPORTANT

If any warning light doesn't work, a different warning light should go on — the one in your *head*. Someone may have tampered with the car to hide a problem.

Tip Provided by
Michael D. Butler
AAA Tri County Motor Club

- Check all accessories for proper operation, including lights, wipers, radio, heater and air conditioning. If it's there, make sure it works.
- Make sure the seats, windows and doors all operate properly.

Road Test — Go for a 20-minute drive on roads you're used to, if possible. Look for anything out of the ordinary or just plain uncomfortable:

- Look for any hesitation or roughness in the engine. It should respond quickly to changes in the throttle position.
- Check the transmission shifts. They should be regular, fairly quick and smooth. Look for long, sloppy shifts or unusually harsh shifts.
- Make sure the car handles and rides comfortably. It shouldn't pull, drift or wander. Pay attention to any noises over bumps or on turns.
- Listen for any noises while driving. Pay particular attention to whether those noises change with engine rpm, road speed or gear range.
- Check the brakes for proper feel and to make sure they stop quickly without pulling or grabbing. Listen for any noises while braking.

Possible Rough Service — It should be no surprise that certain demographics usually are associated with treating their cars rougher than others. While there are no absolutes here, there are a few red flags you might want to avoid:

- Overly expensive or complex aftermarket sound system. This may include a booster or equalizer and really big, expensive speakers.
- Chrome or other decorative replacement components under the hood
- Fancy chrome replacement pedal pads, door lock buttons or other decorative items
- Expensive, flashy wheels
- Raised-letter tires that may be wider than normal
- Noisy exhaust
- Air shocks on cars that really have no need for them
- Gaudy pin striping or racing stripes

Have it Checked Professionally

Even the most critical set of eyes won't see everything on a car — especially with the car sitting on a car lot. That's why, before you even think about spending a great deal of money, you always should have the car checked by your regular repair shop.

The car's owner or salesman won't let you have the car checked? Pass on it — they're hiding something. There are plenty of good cars out there, so there's no reason to take on someone else's headache.

Any good repair shop should be able to examine a used car for you. Their inspections should duplicate yours and then go a step further. Here are some of the items a professional used-car inspection should include:

Under the Hood Examination — The technician should look for any discrepancies under the hood:

- All maintenance items, to make sure the car has been maintained properly
- Any missing or disabled components
- Any specific problems that will have to be addressed immediately
- New parts or recent repairs that could indicate a larger problem
- A test of the charging and starting system

Undercarriage Check — With the car in the air, the technician can check for additional problems that weren't immediately obvious on the ground:

- Signs of an accident or flood damage
- Extreme rust or wear on the body, chassis or suspension
- Any type of leaks
- The condition of the exhaust and brake system

Safety Inspection — If the state has an inspection process in place, it should be performed even if the car isn't actually due for it. If there is no inspection process in place, a safety inspection should include checking all of these items:

- All outside lights
- Doors and windows
- Windshield wipers and washers
- Suspension and steering
- Brakes, including removing all four wheels and examining the brakes visually
- Exhaust

Computer System Scan — The technician should connect a scan tool to the car's computer system and retrieve any diagnostic trouble codes stored in memory. If possible, he also should scan the system's serial data for improper signals (not every computer system allows you to do this).

Emissions Check — Exhaust emissions provide a wealth of information about the engine's mechanical condition, the ignition system and the fuel system. Any indication of a problem should be examined to identify its source.

Powertrain Check — This includes the engine, transmission and differential:

- A complete scope check of the engine operation, including a cylinder balance test
- Engine vacuum check

NOTICE

This is a situation when the mileage dictates the level of the checks. A car with 8,000 miles probably won't require too much in the way of in-depth engine diagnostic checks, while one with 80,000 miles should receive a more thorough examination.

- Blowby from the crankcase
- Transmission engagement and operation

Road Test — During a diagnostic road test, the technician should drive the car under all sorts of conditions, while looking for anything unusual, including:

- Handling problems
- Noises
- Misfires or roughness
- Shifting problems

Once the checks are completed, the shop should provide you with a written list of the results, along with an estimate for any repairs necessary or any items that will need service soon. Armed with that list, you may be able to go back to the car lot or car owner and negotiate a better deal. Or you may decide that the repairs are just too extensive and pass on the car altogether.

Of course, no shop is going to do all this for free. Expect to pay $100 or more for a thorough examination. But that's a small price to pay for the peace of mind you'll get by knowing the car you're buying passed a used-car inspection.

Warranties

Even the most careful checks won't guarantee the car you buy will remain trouble-free in the years ahead. Let's face it, even new cars have problems. That's why many people prefer to buy their used cars from a car dealer instead of a private owner. Most dealers provide at least some level of warranty on their used cars.

Of course, warranties differ from dealer to dealer. Some provide full coverage for 12 months or 12,000 miles. Others only offer a 50-50 powertrain warranty. That is, they only cover 50 percent of the repair on the engine, transmission or differential. The rest is left for you to pay.

But even the best used-car warranties are painfully short when compared with the expected life of a car. That's why you may want to consider purchasing an aftermarket warranty to protect yourself from unexpected expenses.

Aftermarket warranties are warranties you purchase to cover your car against unforeseen expenses. This isn't a unique concept. Go out and purchase a new VCR or washing machine, and one of the first things they'll try to sell you is an extended warranty. While the conventional wisdom says these warranties on home appliances aren't a good investment, your car is an entirely different matter.

That's mostly due to cost. Cars cost more than VCRs and so do their repairs. What's more, when you go to replace that VCR in a couple of years, chances are the cost for a similar unit will be half what you paid originally. Not so with cars. Each year the average price of new cars rises, and that drags the price of good used cars up with it.

So an aftermarket warranty can be a good investment for the typical car owner. The question is, where can you get one? Most car dealers offer some type of aftermarket warranty, but those warranties differ from one company to the next. Some allow you to go anywhere to have your car repaired; others require you to bring the car back to them. Some have larger deductibles than others. Make sure you read the policy carefully before you lay down your hard-earned dollars.

Another place you can go to is your local AAA office. AAA offers a few different warranty plans to extend the manufacturer's warranty on your new car or to cover your used-car purchase, and these warranty plans may prove to be a real bargain compared to others offered by other sources.

Of course, every aftermarket warranty plan has specific requirements, and the AAA plans are no exception. These plans are only available for cars with less than 50,000 miles, and the car must pass a AAA clinic inspection. But for protection and peace of mind, an extended warranty is a great investment. Contact your local AAA office for the specific details on its extended warranty program.

Appendix A
Websites

&

Appendix B
Glossary

Websites

The Internet is a great place to get information or to shop for just about anything. Here's a list — by no means complete — of some automotive websites you might find of interest. AAA cannot guarantee these sites, nor does AAA necessarily agree with their content.

aaa.com — AAA's website. Just enter your ZIP code, and this site will direct you to your local AAA club site.

alldata.com — The professional source for online automotive information now offers single-car subscriptions for the do-it-yourselfer.

autoaccessory.com — Low-cost seat covers, floor mats and other accessories.

automotiveinteriors.com — Custom seat covers, carpets, etc.

autopedia.com — A great source of information, from technical to where to buy your next car online. It includes several bulletin boards to post your questions.

autoshop-online.com — Expert repair advice, tech tips and an introductory automotive course.

car-stuff.com — A list of links to automotive sites, from buying guides to automotive museums.

cartalk.cars.com — National Public Radio's own auto advice radio show online. If you haven't heard this show yet, you should tune in to your local NPR station.

jcwhitney.com — For years, the JC Whitney catalog has been the source for low-cost parts, accessories and supplies, and now it's available online.

napaonline.com — Online auto parts store. AAA members receive a discount when this site is accessed through aaa.com and a purchase is made.

nhtsa.gov/cars/problems — National archive of recalls, service bulletins, reviews and complaints.

Glossary

A

Accumulator – Device that stores extra refrigerant and prevents liquid refrigerant from reaching the compressor.

Air filter – Element designed to remove dust and dirt from air entering the engine.

Alignment – Process of adjusting the angles of the wheels to provide proper handling and tire wear.

Alternator – Generator that creates direct current to keep the battery charged; present-day terminology.

Antifreeze – Coolant additive that prevents water from freezing at -32 degrees F; often used to characterize coolant; outdated terminology.

Antilock brake system – Computerized control system designed to prevent wheels from locking during hard braking.

Antirust – Additive designed to neutralize acids in the coolant and provide additional lubrication for the water pump; a good way to extend coolant life.

Axle – A metal shaft that transfers torque from the differential to the wheels.

B

Backfire – A pop or loud bang from under the hood or the tailpipe, usually created when combustion takes place with the combustion chamber open.

Ball joint – A ball-and-socket joint that allows the suspension to move up and down, while still being able to turn the wheels.

Band – A friction device used in automatic transmissions designed to wrap around a drum, holding it to the case.

Battery – Storage device for electrical power.

Battery cable – Heavy wire that provides power from the battery to the rest of the car.

Battery terminal – The exposed ends of a battery that provide voltage when connected to a circuit.

Blower motor – Electrical motor that blows air over the heater core and evaporator to warm or cool the passenger compartment.

Brake caliper – Actuator for disk brake system; presses disk brake pads against brake rotor to provide friction to stop the wheel.

Brake drum – Rotating part of the drum brake system connected to wheels; brake shoes press against the drum to create friction to stop the wheel.

Brake fluid – Fluid used to transfer movement from the brake pedal through the system to apply the brakes.

Brake rotor – Flat plate connected to the wheels. Disc brake pads press against the rotor to create friction and stop the wheel.

Brake shoes — Friction component of drum brake system.

Bucking — Rapid, repetitive power loss, causing the car to stutter, usually under load.

C

Camshaft — A long shaft made up of a series of egg-shaped sections. As it rotates, it raises and lowers part of the valve train, which causes the valves to open and close.

Carbon dioxide — Byproduct of complete combustion.

Carbon monoxide — Byproduct of combustion without adequate oxygen levels; extremely harmful exhaust emission.

Carburetor — An air/fuel delivery meter that uses the flow of air through the engine to control engine rpm and fuel mixture.

Catalytic converter — Exhaust emissions device that breaks down harmful exhaust emissions into carbon dioxide, nitrogen and water.

Cetane — A diesel fuel rating of how quickly the fuel burns. The higher the rating, the slower and more controlled the fuel burns.

Chassis — Frame of a car, which the body, suspension and powertrain mount to.

Chlorofluorocarbon — Chemical compound shown to damage the Earth's ozone layer; R12 is a chlorofluorocarbon.

Choke — A valve at the top of the carburetor designed to richen mixtures for easier cold starting and running.

Clutch disc — A splined disc with friction material on either side. The splines ride on the input shaft for the manual transmission; the friction material rides between the flywheel and the pressure plate.

Clutch pack — A series of small friction disks designed to grab or release a component by applying oil pressure to a piston. The piston presses against the clutches, causing them to grab.

Coil spring — See *spring*

Cold start injector — A special fuel injector that provides additional fuel to the intake during cold starting; only used on some fuel systems.

Combustion chamber — The area in the cylinder between the top of the piston and the cylinder head where the air/fuel mixture actually ignites and burns.

Compression engine — An internal combustion engine that creates power without using a spark to fire the air/fuel mixture; another term for a diesel engine.

Compressor — A pump that moves refrigerant through the A/C system.

Compressor clutch — A magnetic device that couples the compressor pulley with the compressor shaft, which turns the compressor on and off.

Condenser — Heat exchanger in front of the car that releases heat from the A/C refrigerant to the outside air.

Constant velocity joint – A flexible joint that transfers power while flexing back and forth, or up and down. This lets front-wheel drive cars send power to the front wheels while still steering the car.

Coolant – Liquid that carries heat away from the engine and releases it to the outside air; provides additional protection from corrosion, freezing and overheating.

Cooling fan – A fan that pulls air past the radiator to keep the engine from overheating at low vehicle speeds. The cooling fan becomes ineffective at about 40 mph.

Crank; cranking – Operating an engine with an electrical motor to enable it to start.

Crankshaft – A series of offset levers that connect to the pistons through connecting rods. As the pistons move, they turn the crankshaft, which turns combustion into torque to drive the car.

Cylinder – A round chamber for the piston to travel through.

Cylinder head – A casting that mounts on top of the cylinders. This provides the top of the combustion chamber, a housing for the valves, and channels for the intake and exhaust.

D

Desiccant – Drying agent. A/C systems use a desiccant to absorb moisture that gets into the system.

Detonation – More correctly, predetonation; slang for ping or engine knock.

Dex-Cool^{TM} – Brand name for an extended-life coolant.

Diagnostic trouble code – Numerical code that indicates problems in the computer system.

Diesel – An internal combustion engine that fires without the use of an ignition system. Diesel engines use high compression to fire the mixture in the cylinders.

Dieseling – Run-on that occurs when a gasoline engine is idling too high. The engine seems to continue running after you turn the ignition off.

Differential – A geared unit that allows the wheels on opposite sides of the car to turn at different speeds. This is necessary while the car is turning.

Direct drive – A condition where the transmission connects the engine to the differential directly, without altering the gear ratio.

Disk brake pads – Friction component of disk brake system.

Distributor – An early mechanical device that controls the ignition spark and delivers it to the proper cylinders at the right moment.

Distributor cap – A plastic cap that provides a path for the spark to go to each individual cylinder.

Distributorless ignition – An electronic ignition system that creates spark without the use of a mechanical distributor using signals from electrical sensors on the crankshaft.

Do-it-yourselfer — Someone who repairs or services his or her own car instead of taking it to a repair shop.

Driveshaft — A shaft that transfers power from the transmission to the differential on rear-wheel drive cars.

Dynamometer — Set of rollers designed to provide a load to simulate actual driving conditions while in the shop.

E

Electrolysis — A chemical process for developing electricity; the wear that takes place in a system consisting of dissimilar metals in an acid matrix.

Engine block — The large part of the engine that houses the cylinders and water jacket. The pistons, crankshaft and camshaft all reside in the engine block.

Engine control module — Electronic controller; computer that controls engine operation only.

Engine coolant temperature sensor — Sensor that monitors the temperature of the engine coolant.

Ethylene glycol — Chemical name for standard coolant.

Evaporator — Heat exchanger that transfers heat from the passenger compartment to the A/C refrigerant.

Exhaust gas recirculation valve — Valve that allows a metered amount of exhaust into the intake to reduce combustion temperature. This prevents ping or knock and lowers NOx levels.

Exhaust manifold — A steel or cast series of channels that collect exhaust from the cylinders and direct it to the exhaust system.

Expansion valve — Variable orifice that forces refrigerant to expand and take on heat. This makes the refrigerant very cold.

F

Fan clutch — A liquid-filled coupling that allows the cooling fan to turn more slowly than the engine rpm; improves economy and reduces engine noise.

Fast idle — A condition used during cold operation to increase idle speed so the engine will run with a richer mixture.

Federal Test Procedure — Test used by the federal government to certify new cars for use on the road.

Firewall — Car's body panel between the engine and passenger compartments.

Flywheel — Plate mounted to the back of the engine with a gear for the starter to turn the engine.

Freeze plug — A small cup designed to blow out if the coolant freezes to prevent damage to the engine. Freeze plugs often rust and cause coolant leaks.

Fuel cell — A catalyst that creates electricity by combining hydrogen and oxygen into water.

Fuel injector – A small valve, usually electrically controlled, that controls the amount of fuel entering the engine.

Fuel pump – A mechanical or electric device that transfers fuel from the tank to the carburetor or injectors at the proper pressure.

G

Gear ratio – The difference in the number of rotations between the engine crankshaft and the transmission output shaft, which allows the transmission to vary speed and torque.

Generator – Magnetic windings that the engine turns to create a voltage to keep the battery charged; outdated terminology.

Glow plug – A small electric heater in the cylinder on some diesel engines that provides additional heat during cold starting.

H

Head gasket – A composite or metal shim that fits between the cylinder head and engine block to seal the two surfaces.

Heater core – A small radiator that provides heat from the engine coolant to warm the passenger compartment.

Hesitation – A momentary loss of power during engine operation.

Hydrocarbons – Raw, unburned gasoline; reacts with sunlight to create photochemical smog.

Hydrometer – Low-cost device for measuring coolant protection level.

I

Idle – The speed the engine runs with the car stopped and your foot off the gas.

Ignition coil – A step-up transformer that turns 12 volts into a high-voltage, low-amperage spark to fire the cylinders.

Ignition module – An electronic device that energizes and de-energizes the ignition coil to create a spark for engine operation.

Ignition rotor – A plastic device that sits inside the distributor cap, which directs the spark from the center of the cap to the individual cylinders.

Ignition switch – Electrical switch that enables the driver to start and operate the engine; the "key."

IM240 – Emissions test based on the Federal Test Procedure.

Induction system – Part of the engine that induces air into the engine; includes the carburetor or throttle body and the intake manifold.

Intake air temperature sensor – Sensor that monitors the temperature of the incoming air.

Intake manifold – A cast series of channels that directs air – and sometimes fuel – to the individual cylinders.

Internal combustion — Literally "burns inside." A type of engine that creates power by burning a fuel internally. Most cars on the road today use internal combustion engines, including those using gasoline and diesel fuels.

K, L

Knock — A noise caused by combustion occurring too quickly; also called a ping or detonation.

Leaf spring — See *spring*

Lifter — A small, hardened-metal cylinder that rides along the camshaft to open the valves.

Lug nut — A threaded nut used to hold the wheel onto the axle.

M

MacPherson strut — A type of suspension that combines the spring, shock absorber and spindle in one unit.

Malfunction indicator lamp — Warning lamp on the dashboard the computer uses to indicate problems in the computer system.

Manifold absolute pressure sensor — Pressure sensor connected to the intake manifold. The computer uses this signal to determine engine load.

Manual clutch — A coupling device that allows the driver to engage and disengage the engine and manual transmission. When engaged, the clutch transfers power from the engine to the transmission; when disengaged, the driver can shift gears or allow the vehicle to come to a stop without stalling the engine.

Mass airflow sensor — Measures the amount of air entering the engine to provide the computer with a load measurement.

Master cylinder — Hydraulic control device that converts the force from the driver's foot to hydraulic force in the brake system.

Miss; misfire — Failure to cause the mixture in the combustion chamber to burn.

Motor mount — Usually a rubber or hydraulic device that holds the engine in place while absorbing engine vibrations.

N, O

Neutral safety switch — Switch that prevents the starter from operating in any transmission range except park or neutral.

Octane — A gasoline rating of how quickly the fuel burns. The higher the rating, the slower and more controlled the fuel burns.

Odometer — Device on the instrument panel to record miles traveled.

Oil filter — An element that strains dirt and particles out of the engine oil.

Oil pump — A pump that forces engine oil through the engine to lubricate the moving parts.

Oil pan — The tray that bolts to the bottom of the engine to collect engine oil to be pumped back through the engine.

Orifice tube — Fixed orifice that forces A/C refrigerant to expand and take on heat. This makes the refrigerant very cold.

Oxides of nitrogen — Product of excessive combustion temperature; extremely harmful exhaust emission.

Oxygen sensor — Indicates the level of unburned fuel in the exhaust so the computer can adjust the air/fuel level.

P

Ping — See *knock*

Piston — A round cup that slides through the cylinders to create the flow of air through the engine and transfer the energy of combustion to the crankshaft.

Play — Looseness, usually in the steering; a condition where turning the steering wheel doesn't affect the direction of the car.

Positraction — A type of differential that limits the difference in speed between the right and left wheel. This helps prevent the car from spinning its wheels and getting stuck on ice or snow.

Power booster — Vacuum or hydraulic device designed to amplify the force the driver applies to the brake pedal to make braking easier.

Powertrain control module — Electronic controller; computer that controls engine and transmission operation.

Pre-ignition — See *knock*

Pressure plate — A metal plate with springs and levers. The springs hold the clutch disc to the flywheel; the levers allow the driver to disengage the clutch.

Pressure regulator — A device that controls fuel pressure to the fuel injectors.

Propylene glycol — Chemical name for environmentally safe coolant.

R

R12 — Old-style refrigerant; shown to cause damage to the Earth's ozone layer.

R134a — New refrigerant; designed to be safe for the Earth's ozone layer.

Radial — A method of constructing a tire where the belts are aligned in a fashion that provides additional traction beyond those of earlier designs.

Radiator — A series of vanes and fins that conducts heat from the coolant and allows outside air to carry it away.

Receiver/dryer — Device that stores excess refrigerant and contains a desiccant to remove moisture from the system.

Refractometer — Professional device for measuring coolant protection level.

Refrigerant — Chemical used to transfer heat by taking advantage of the laws of physics.

S

Serpentine belt — A wide, flat drive belt that drives multiple accessories used on most new cars.

Shimmy — Unwanted, repetitive, back-and-forth movement in the steering usually caused by wear or looseness.

Shock absorber — A hydraulic piston that stops the suspension from bouncing.

Sidewall — The side part of the tire that connects the tread to the wheel.

Slip — A condition where the clutch or automatic transmission seems to disengage and allows the engine to rev up without transferring power to the wheels.

Solenoid — Large capacity relay designed to energize the starter when you turn the key.

Spark engine — Any internal combustion engine that creates power by using a spark to fire the air/fuel mixture. This includes engines that use gasoline, propane and natural gas.

Spark plug — A small, ceramic device that uses the spark from the ignition system to fire the mixture inside the combustion chamber.

Speedometer — Device on the instrument panel to display current vehicle speed.

Spindle — Shaft that holds the wheel at the proper angle, while allowing it to rotate freely.

Sport-utility vehicle — Sort of a cross between a truck and a station wagon; highly popular vehicles, larger than a typical car, but not quite a truck or van.

Spring — Device used to hold the car up while providing a cushion against bumps or dips in the road. Springs come in three main types: coil, leaf and torsion bar. Some cars use a system of air bags instead of springs.

Stall — A condition where the engine shuts off, usually when coming to a stop.

Starter — Electrical motor that cranks the engine, enabling it to start.

Starter drive — Gear that engages the starter with the flywheel, allowing the starter to crank the engine.

Steering box — A worm gear and spur gear that allows the driver to turn the wheels.

Steering pump — A pump that provides hydraulic pressure for power steering, which makes it easier to turn the steering.

Steering rack — A type of steering box that uses a flat "rack" gear and a spur gear to turn the wheels; usually considered more responsive than a steering box.

Stop-leak — An additive designed to seal leaks in the cooling system; only to be used as an emergency measure, not a permanent repair.

Stumble — An erratic roughness in the engine, usually at idle.

Sump – The pan at the bottom of the automatic transmission that collects fluid and holds it there for the transmission to use.

Surge – A repetitive increase and decrease in power, usually during acceleration.

T

Terminal ends – Metal clamps or flanges that connect the battery cables to the battery.

Thermostat – A valve that keeps coolant from flowing until it reaches about 200 degrees F to allow the engine to warm up faster.

Throttle body – Part of the fuel injection system that houses the throttle plate and controls the amount of air that flows through the engine.

Throttle position sensor – Measures the angle of the throttle plate, which the computer uses to determine engine load.

Throwout bearing – A flat bearing that rides against the pressure plate, which allows the driver to disengage the clutch while the engine's running.

Tie rod end – A small ball-and-socket joint used as part of the steering linkage.

Timing belt – A belt that runs between the crankshaft and camshaft to turn the camshaft and keep the two in the correct relative positions; used on some vehicles instead of a timing chain.

Timing chain – A chain that runs between the crankshaft and camshaft to turn the camshaft and keep the two in the correct relative positions; used on some vehicles instead of a timing belt.

Tire rotation – To switch the tires to a different corner of the car, allowing them to wear more evenly.

Torque – A measurement of force. The drivetrain converts the engine's power to torque at the wheels.

Torque converter – A fluid coupling that mounts between the engine and automatic transmission. The torque converter drives the car with oil movement. Since there's no mechanical connection, the driver can stop the car without stalling the engine.

Torque converter clutch – A mechanical connection within the torque converter that eliminates slip at higher speeds. This prevents the converter from creating additional heat and increases fuel mileage slightly.

Torsion bar – See *spring.*

Transmission control module – Electronic controller; computer that controls transmission operation only.

Transmission filter – An element that strains the fluid in the transmission to remove dirt particles, clutch material or metal shavings, and prevents them from going through the transmission.

Transmission fluid – A multipurpose fluid necessary for the transmission to operate. The transmission fluid lubricates and cools the transmission while also applying clutches and even providing the power transfer between the engine and transmission.

Tread – The part of the tire that contacts the road. Treads provide traction and special handling.

U, V, W

Universal joint – A cross-shaped set of pivots that allow the transmission and differential to operate at different levels.

Valve – A round plate with a shaft attached. The plate opens and closes the intake or exhaust ports to the combustion chamber to control flow through the engine.

V-belt – Thin, V-shaped drive belt that usually drives only one or two accessories.

Vehicle speed sensor – Provides a signal that the computer can use to read road speed.

Vibration – A problem in the steering or suspension usually caused by a wheel imbalance.

Viscosity – Resistance of a liquid to flow; thickness of a liquid. When referring to oils, higher viscosity – in most general terms – means thicker. In that case, we say the oil is "more viscous."

Voltage regulator – Electronic device that controls the charging voltage from the alternator to prevent it from overcharging.

Wander – Steering problem that causes the car to alter its direction randomly.

Water jacket – The channels through the engine that coolant flows through, to carry heat away.

Water pump – A pump that keeps coolant flowing through the cooling system.

Wheel alignment – See *alignment.*

Wheel balancing – A process of finding the heavy spots on a tire and adding weight to the opposite sides to overcome those heavy spots.

Wheel cylinder – Actuator for drum brake system; presses the brake shoes out against the brake drum to create friction and stop the wheel.

Wheel lug – A threaded stud that enables the wheel to be held onto the axle using a lug nut.

Wheel well – Inner fender that surrounds the wheel to prevent dirt and rocks from launching up into the engine compartment or trunk.

Windshield – The front safety glass on a car.

Abbreviations and Acronyms

ABS – Antilock brake system

A/C – Air conditioning

API – American Petroleum Institute

ATF – Automatic transmission fluid

BTDC – Before top dead center

CAFE – Corporate average fuel economy

CAT – Catalytic converter

CFC – Chlorofluorocarbon

CO – Carbon monoxide

CO_2 – Carbon dioxide

CVT – Continuously variable transmission

DIY or DIYer – Do-it-yourselfer

DTC – Diagnostic trouble code

ECM – Engine control module

ECT – Engine coolant temperature sensor

EGO – Exhaust gas oxygen sensor

EGR – Exhaust gas recirculation valve

EPA – Environmental Protection Agency

EVAP – Evaporative emissions system

FTP – Federal Test Procedure

H_2 – Hydrogen

H_2O – Water

HC – Hydrocarbons

HEGO – Heated exhaust gas oxygen sensor

IAC – Idle air control solenoid

KPH – Kilometers per hour

MAF – Mass airflow sensor

MAP – Manifold absolute pressure sensor

MIL – Malfunction indicator lamp

MPH – Miles per hour

NOx – Oxides of nitrogen; nitrogen oxides

O_2 – Oxygen

PCM – Powertrain control module

PCV – Positive crankcase ventilation valve

RPM – Revolutions per minute

SAE – Society of Automotive Engineers

SUV – Sport-utility vehicle

TCC – Torque converter clutch

TCM – Transmission control module

TDC – Top dead center

TPS – Throttle position sensor

TSB – Technical service bulletin

VSS – Vehicle speed sensor

Index

A

AAA, 3, 22, 23, 28, 29, 65, 71, 83, 86, 87, 88, 104, 120, 153, 155, 159, 161, 172, 211, 212, 215, 219, 230, 232, 236, 238, 170
ABS, 170
aaa.com, 230, 238
ABS Light, 21
A/C system, 52, 177-185
acceleration, 71
Adding Oil to the Engine, 50
additives, 122
A-frame, 129
AIR, 190
air bags, 33
air conditioning and heating systems, 179
air conditioning compressor, 52
Air Conditioning System Maintenance, 184
Air Filter, 74
air pressure, 155
alignment
    front-end, 139
    wheel, 137
all-wheel drive. *See* four-wheel drive
alternator, 98, 100
American Petroleum Institute, 46
ammeters, 99
antifreeze, 82
antilock brakes, 169, 170
Approved Auto Repair Program, 219
ASE, 218
ATRA or ATSG, 218
auto technicians, 220
automatic transmission fluid, 117
    checking the fluid level, 118
automatic transmissions, 112
    service procedures, 121
auxiliary coolers, 122

B

Balance and alignment, 153
bands, 112
battery, 93
    buying a new, 95
    cell, 94
    dry cell, 93
    how to jump-start, 104
    terminal, 96
    wet-cell, 93

battery terminals, 94
Belt Wear, 54
Body Damage, 231
brake
    changing the fluid, 172
    checking fluid, 173
    fluid, 167
    fluid rating, 171
    hydraulic systems, 167, 169
    shoes or pads, 167
    system maintenance, 173
    system overview, 165
Brake Light, 21
brake shoes and pads, 167
buying a used car, 229

C

car
    cleaning, 199
    cleaning exterior, 200
    cleaning it yourself, 199
    polishing the finish, 202
    professional cleaning, 198
    protecting the vinyl, 203
    touching up the paint, 201
    waxing, 203
Carbon Monoxide (CO), 192
Carbureted Engines, 74
carburetor, 69
car's computer system, 65
CAT, 190
Cell Phone, 212
Cetane, 72
CFC's, 181
Changing a Flat, Step by Step, 159
Charging System, 98
Charging System Light, 20
Check Engine , 21
Checking Power Steering Fluid Level, 136
Checking the Oil, 48
Checking the Tire Pressure, 154
Checking Tire Condition, 157
chlorofluorocarbons, 181
Choosing a Repair Facility, 217
Cleaning the Exterior, 200
cleaning your car, 197
climate, 151
climate control systems, 179
closed loop feedback system, 62
clutch, 115
    cable, 115

checking a slipping, 116
    make last longer, 117
    packs, 112
    pedal, 113
    service procedures, 115
Cold Cranking Amps, 96
combination valves, 169
Compression engine, 41
compression stroke, 40
computer metering, 70
Computer System Scan, 234
condenser, 180
continuously variable transmission, 109
coolant, 81
    level, 84
    protection, 85
cooling system, 81
Cranking amps, 96
crankshaft, 41
CVT, 109
cylinder, 40, 41, 45, 52, 56, 61, 70, 81, 93, 130, 167, 168, 169, 173, 174, 175, 234

D

Dashboard Indicators, 99
Dex-Cool^{TM}, 82
diagnostic time, 225
diesel engine, 41
diesel fuel additives, 73
differentials, 123
Dispute Resolution, 219
distributorless ignition system, 61
DOT number, 147, 150
Drive belts, 51, 52
drivetrain, 109
driving conditions
    normal, 26
    severe, 26
Driving Practices, 34
Drum Brake Assembly, 166
Dry Boiling Point, 171
Dynamometer testing, 190

E

EGR, 190
Electric Motors, 42
electrical system, 93
    cell, 94
electronic fuel injection systems, 70
emergency brake, 169

The One That Does It All

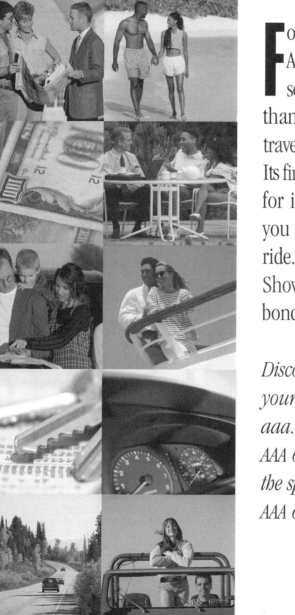

For years, people have turned to AAA for their emergency road service needs. But AAA is more than just towing. Access to AAA's travel services can give you the world. Its financial services can help you pay for it. And AAA insurance can give you the peace of mind to enjoy the ride. Plus AAA gives you exclusive Show Your Card & Save® offers, bail bond benefits and much more.

Discover the ways AAA can simplify your life. Call 800-JOINAAA, visit aaa.com or stop by your nearest AAA office <u>today</u> to find out about the specific products and services AAA offers.

The AAA Auto Guide series is designed to help you with all aspects of vehicle ownership and use, including car buying and car care. These comprehensive how-to guides give you a road map to navigate potentially frustrating experiences while helping you save time and money. Each book in the Auto Guide series feature practical tools like worksheets, checklists, charts and illustrations to show you how to get the most out of your car.

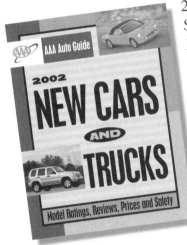

2002 New Cars and Trucks
$14.95 US $22.95 CDN
ISBN: 1-56251-615-9
Reviews and ratings, safety features, reliability, prices and specs. Updated annually.

Buying or Leasing a Car
$14.95 US $21.95 CDN
ISBN: 1-56251-577-2
Includes how to buy a new or used car, sell your trade-in, and use the Internet for research.

Available at participating bookstores, AAA club offices, www.aaa.com or by calling toll-free 877-AAA-BOOK.